mDecks Series

Mapping Tonal Harmony Workbook 5

Chords, functions and progressions in every key

Mapping blues I7 IV7. Additional minor mode functions
The bIIMaj7 subdominant minor and its related IIm7-V7

Ariel J. Ramos

This page intentionally leftt blank

Table of Contents

Introductory Chapters

Worksheets by key

This page intentionally leftt blank

Prerequisites

To take full advantage of these books, the student must know:

- intervals and how to classify them into minor, major, augmented, etc

- have a good understanding of basic chord structures and chord symbols

- be able to play a harmonic instrument (preferably piano and/or guitar) at an intermediate level

- Key signatures for all keys, major and minor is also required

Some knowledge of harmony, harmonic concepts and progressions is recommended, although not required, since these books are meant to be used as supplementary material in the study of tonal harmony.

Evaluation Quiz

Test your level by answering the following quiz. If you are able to answer most of the questions, you are ready to embark in the study of Mapping Tonal Harmony Vol. 1

1. What is an interval?
2. What is a major third?
3. What is a perfect fifth?
4. How do you change a perfect fourth into a tritone?
5. C to Ab is a _____ (interval?)
6. A tritone divides the octave into _____ equal parts.
7. Can you write and play a E triad?
8. Can you write and play a Am7b5?
9. What is the order of flats and sharps in the key signatures?
10. A key signature with 4 sharps indicates the the key of _____ major, or _____ minor.
11. Can you play any major and minor triad in all three inversions?
12. Can you play all major and minor seventh chords in all four inversions?
13. Do you know your major scales?

Introduction

The volumes in the **Mapping Tonal Harmony** collection have been envisioned as auxiliary material in the study of Tonal Harmony. The main objective of these books is to provide the student, teachers, composers and/or songwriters with a tool that will aid them in hearing, analyzing, foreseeing, and composing harmonic progressions without struggle, in all keys alike.

Most students have a pretty good understanding of how harmony works, only in certain keys. A beginner student may know that in the key of C the V7 is G7, that C7 is also the V7 in the key of F and probably that the progression G7 – C produce a cadence where all tension in the G7 chord is released by the C triad, exactly as in the progression C7 – F, but they would have to think for a while before telling what that cadence in the key of Gb is.

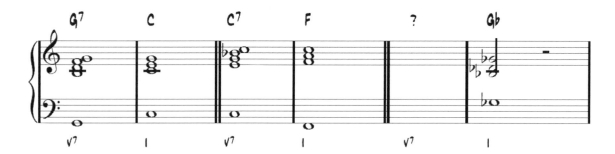

A more advanced student may have a set of chords or cadences he/she fancies, such as Eb/G - A7, or Dm7 – Db7#11 – C69, or Bb – Ab – C, without understanding the origin of these chords or the functions they might be playing in a certain key. A student would hear and like the sound without knowing the possible functional interpretation (or context) and, consequently have a hard time exploiting/hearing these sounds in other keys or passages in a song.

It is remarkable though, how perception changes once a link is made between the chord and a chosen harmonic function. As soon as one learns that the Eb/G could be considered a Neapolitan Sixth chord in the key of Dm, that can precede the V7, which wants to resolve to the Im, many possible outcomes arise, since assigning a function to that Eb/G chord puts it in context, thus:

- The Eb/G – A7 could now resolve to Dm as expected:

Eb/G	A7	Dm
N6	V7	Im

- or delayed by a cadential six-four Im64 (or Im/5, in this case Dm/A) :

Eb/G	Dm/A	A7	Dm
N6	I64	V7	Im

- or resolve deceptively to a Bb major chord the bVI in the key of Dm :

Eb/G	A7	Bb	
N6	V7	bVI	

- or resolve to a D major triad instead of the expected Dm.

Eb/G	A7	D	
N6	V7	I	

- or even to a D7 as a secondary dominant of the IV minor (which would probably resolve to Gm)

Eb/G	A7	D7	Gm	
N6	V7	V7/IV	IVm	

Any of these progressions are still in the key of D minor (or just D). They all belong to the same set of harmonic functions in that key. The student should, not only have a good knowledge of many harmonic functions, but also the respective chord for each of these functions in any key. It is of little significance to know that V7 – I is a perfect authentic cadence if we cannot hear it and/or we do not know the V7 chord's name in all keys. In other words, **key preferences and harmonic progressions should be decided by choice rather by limitation**.

All maps, progression examples, exercises, and songs in these books, were designed to improve and expand the student's view of the harmonic surroundings around each and every tonal center.

Mapping Tonal Harmony

In order to understand what makes tonal harmony a good candidate for mapping, we should first take a close look at its properties and rules.

Harmony is an artificial concept derived from the assumption that the simultaneity of two or more melodic lines creates a vertical music entity, and that it is possible to analyze, classify, and establish rules and behavior patterns for such entity. Harmony, in the hands of a composer, takes a step further becoming the source for those melodic lines.

Tonal, or functional harmony, has evolved into a complex system and is the base for almost all contemporary music, from Classical, Romantic to Rock, Gospel, Pop, New Age, and Jazz. Most of the rules in harmony are rooted in the treatment of consonance and dissonance, which gives the intervals of the **fifth** and **third** a key role in the system. The **fifth** governs the movement of the bass or root of the chords, while the **third** is the building block for those chords (which are built by stacking thirds).

A chord type and its denomination is a consequence of the kind of thirds that are stacked to form it. For example: A **major triad** consists in a major plus a minor third. A **minor seventh (m7) chord** is a minor 3rd + major 3rd + minor 3rd. Even when a chord is inverted (such as EGC) we will arrange the notes in thirds (CEG) and consider the inverted chords as a transformation of the root position chord (C in first inversion, or C/E)

Any piece of music conceived using tonal harmony could be analyzed and described as sequences of chords we call **Harmonic Progressions**. Although in principle, a harmonic progression could be a sequence of any type of chords in any order, the search for balance between consonance and dissonance (tension and release) has yield a set of most often used progressions and expected harmonic functions paths.

The most important principle in tonal harmony is the existence of a pole, a point of maximum relaxation we call **Tonic**. Although the tonic may change many times in one song (event called modulation), a tonic should be present at any given moment. The tonic is a target, a resting point, and sometimes the starting point for any tonal piece. All harmonic paths are expected to find a way back to it. Once the tonic has been established, a set of **harmonic functions** arise (such as the dominant V7 or the subdominant IV, etc.). These harmonic functions have a specific sound and an expected resolution path.

A function is always linked to a unique chord type whose root is labeled relative to the tonic (for example IIm7 is a minor seventh chord whose root is a step above the tonic). Although each function "points" to a specific chord relative to the tonic, the opposite is not true; a chord could belong to many different functions in the same key.

In the key of C, Am could be the VIm or the II of V (II of G) which makes the analysis of a harmonic progression only valid in context. In other words, the VIm in the key of C is always Am, but Am does not always play the role of the VIm in C.

Cmaj7		Am7		Dm7	G7	Cmaj7	
Imaj7		VIm7		IIm7	V7	Imaj7	

Cmaj7		Am7	D7	Dm7	G7	Cmaj7	
Imaj7		IIm7/V	V7/V	IIm7	V7	Imaj7	

Diatonic and non-Diatonic Functions

There are two main types of functions in tonal harmony: Diatonic and non-Diatonic.
A function is considered diatonic when all notes in its respective chord belong to the key of the Tonic. All other functions are non-diatonic.

The major diatonic scale can be obtained by stacking six perfect fifths.
In the key of C major (CDEFGAB) the notes F C G D A E B are all a perfect fifth apart.

Since every note in a diatonic chord function must belong to the scale of the tonic, there could be only as many diatonic functions as notes in a scale, thus, there are only seven diatonic chord functions in a key with seven notes.

The diatonic chord functions using triads are:

Major	I	IIm	IIIm	IV	V	VIm	VII°
Natural Minor	Im	II°	bIII	IVm	Vm	bVI	bVII

The diatonic chord functions using sevenths:

Major	IMaj7	IIm7	IIIm7	IVMaj7	V7	VIm7	VIIm7b5
Natural Minor	Im7	IIm7b5	bIIIMaj7	IVm7	Vm7	bVIMaj7	bVII7

The natural minor mode presents several harmonic problems:

1) All chords in the natural minor mode coincide with its relative major mode (staring on the sixth degree), implying that a diatonic chord progression in natural minor could be interpreted as being in its relative major and vice versa
2) The only dominant chord in natural minor is not the V but the bVII7, which should properly resolve to the bIII of this natural minor key
3) The fifth degree is not a dominant chord thus, it does not contain a tritone which means there is not enough tension to create a strong V-I cadence
4) Finally, there is no leading tone to the I. The seventh degree in natural minor is a b7 (the 7th is not diatonic in the natural minor mode)

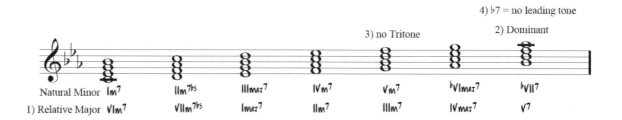

Composers have found a way of solving these issues by altering a few notes in the natural minor. The resulting scales are still considered *diatonic*, although they cannot be constructed by stacking perfect fifths.

The most important transformation is replacing the b7 with the 7, scale known as the **Harmonic Minor**.

The resulting "diatonic" functions for this minor mode are:

Triads	Im	II°	bIII+	IVm	V	bVI	VII°
Sevenths	ImMaj7	IIm7b5	bIII+Maj7	IVm7	V7	bVIMaj7	VII°7

The harmonic minor does not present any of the issues mentioned prior:

1) The chord functions in harmonic minor do not coincide in order or type, with any major key (not even its relative major).
2) The only dominant chord is the V7, resolving as expected, to the tonic.
3) The fifth degree contains a tritone.
4) The leading tone belongs to the harmonic minor scale by definition.

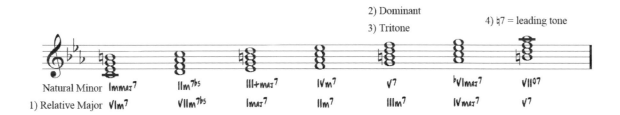

Although the harmonic minor fixes all harmonic issues present in the natural minor, it creates a new melodic one:

There is a melodic gap between the b6 and the 7 which does not exist in the natural minor. A one and a half steps gap is not only a tough skip to hear and sing, but it also affects the uniformity of the scale, which contains whole and half steps only, between any other degrees.

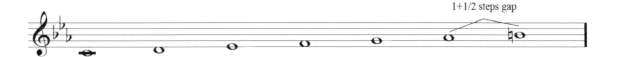

1 whole step

This problem is solved by raising the b6 to 6 yielding the **Melodic Minor**. In this mode the one-and-a-half step gap disappears without affecting the harmonic minor scale's properties.

The "diatonic" functions for the melodic minor mode are:

Triads	Im	IIm	bIII+	IV	V	VI°	VII°
Sevenths	ImMaj7	IIm7	bIII+Maj7	IV7	V7	VIm7b5	VIIm7b5

Again, new issues result from this transformation, mainly with the fourth degree of the scale. There are now two dominant seventh chords: IV7 and V7, both wanting to resolve to a different tonic. Also, the IV is not a minor chord anymore since the b6 degree's characteristic minor sound (Le, or lowered La) has been changed to 6 (La). Consequently, the minor sounding melodic line Le-Sol is gone, and so is the VIm, the IIm7b5, and the VIIo7.

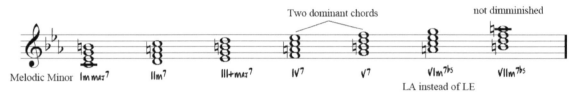

Two dominant chords

not dimminished

Melodic Minor Im maj7   IIm7   III+maj7   IV7   V7   VIm7b5   VIIm7b5

LA instead of LE

Minor Complex Mode

The final and definite solution arrives in the form of a *compound minor mode*, an amalgamation of the three modes: Natural Minor - Harmonic Minor - Melodic Minor, being the harmonic minor the predominant mode in the harmonic treatment of a tonal minor piece.

The most often used "diatonic" chord functions in the minor complex mode are:

Triads	Im	II°	bIII	IVm	V	VIo	bVII VII°
Sevenths	Im7 ImMaj7	IIm7b5	bIIIMaj7	IVm7	V7	bVIMaj7 VIm7b5	bVII7 bVIIMaj7 VII°7

Tonic – Sub-Dominant – Dominant

A further classification of diatonic functions (and several other non-diatonic) could be done by considering the amount of harmonic tension.

Since harmonic tension is a consequence of melodic tension, the same as harmony is a consequence of melody, it is reasonable to assume that a classification of harmonic functions by tension could be somewhat derived from the scale degrees they contain. It is important to notice that this criteria will yield some ambiguous results, in which some other properties of each harmonic function (and the study and analysis of many tonal pieces) will need to be taken into account to find a proper classification.

In tonal harmony, diatonic functions are classified into three regions: **Tonic, Sub-Dominant and Dominant**, being the functions in the Tonic region the most stable and the ones in the Dominant the ones with most tension.

Melodically the most stable degrees are the 1, 3 (b3 in minor) and 5. The most unstable degree is the 7th which resolves half a step up to the tonic, then the 4th resolving a half step down to the 3rd then the b6 resolving half step down to the 5th.

A simple algorithm to classify the functions would be the following:
1) If the diatonic function contains the 7, it is dominant
2) Else, if the diatonic functions contains the 4 or the b6, it is sub-dominant.
3) Else, the diatonic function is tonic.

The resulting sub-sets in major are:

Tonic	I		*			VIm	
Dominant			IIIm*		V7		VII°
Sub-Dominant		IIm		IV			

Notice that the IIIm contains the unstable 7 but also two of the stable degrees (3 and 5) weakening its tension which makes it an ambiguous function.

The resulting sub-sets in the minor complex are:

Tonic	Im		bIII			VI°	
Dominant					V7		VII°
Sub-Dominant		II°		IVm		bVI	bVII*

* A case for placing the bVII in the dominant region will be made later on, in order to gain consistency when mapping the minor diatonic functions.

Why mapping?

We have now defined a focal/resting point called **Tonic** and a set of close related functions known as **Diatonic** (major and/or minor) which have been classified or sorted by levels of tension into the three main harmonic regions: **Tonic, Sub-dominant, Dominant**. Also, any other harmonic function outside the diatonic set has been assigned to a **non-Diatonic** set (a complementary set).

All these sets and subsets, containing harmonic functions, are only dependent on the tonic, and exist for all tonics, thus, every tonic will have the same exact relative functions and the chord names for those functions will be an invariable, once that tonic has been established.
For example: in C, V7/II is always A7, IIm7/IV is always Gm7, etc.

It should be of course that by graphing those functions in a map, based on their classification (sets, subsets, properties, etc) relatively to a tonic, we can create a useful visual representation in any key where we can, not only view a complete picture of all possible harmonic functions, but also, analyze, study and compose harmonic progressions by outlining their paths on the map.

Constructing a Tonal Harmony Map

Designing a tonal map involves the creation of a landscape that is well-defined, logical, easy to navigate, and consistent with common-practice harmonic progressions. In order to achieve such task, it is crucial to find a very basic principle that could act as the map's building block, and is a defining element in tonal harmony.

The best candidate is, without a doubt, the interval of a ***perfect fifth***.

The perfect fifth was the first interval used harmonically; it is the first interval (other than the octave) to appear in the harmonic series; it is the defining interval in the diatonic scale; and it has governed the movement of the root in harmonic progressions since the beginning of tonal harmony.

A standard method of organizing perfects fifths is done by graphing all notes over evenly distributed nodes around a circle, known as the ***Circle of Fifths,*** since the twelve tones in our music system may be obtained by stacking eleven perfects fifths. It also reflects the order of flats and sharps in the key signatures.

In order to standardize the representation of functions over the circle of fifths, we will use the **"Decoding the Circle of Fifths"** system (which is also part of the **mDecks Series**). In this system, structures are clearly notated and easy to analyze.

Graphing vs. Music Notation

Standard Music Notation is a great way of communicating musical ideas to the performer but it is sometimes not very clear if one needs to analyze structures and their properties.

Take a look at this example:

All the intervals in the previous example look very different but in fact they all sound exactly the same. They are all a perfect 5th (at least sound-wise).

Enharmonic spellings (as in the example) will make things very confusing when analyzing intervals in a structure.

Since we will be dealing with Major and Minor triads and sevenths chords in all keys, we will sometimes need a method, such as **graphing**, that can clearly show identical structures, chords and functions in a unique way.

As a graphing tool we will use the "**Decoding the Circle of Fifths**" system (which is part of the **mDecks Series**). In this system, structures are clearly notated and easy to analyze. Combining standard music notation and the "Decoding the Circle of Fifths" system, we can approach and challenge all questions in a better, more effective way.

Enharmonic spelling in these books: Music examples and studies were notated trying to avoid double flats and double sharps (or chord notation where the harmonic function would be, for example, correctly spelled as a Cb instead of B).

Chord Notation
Chords are notated in standard chord notation with tensions, such as Dm7 or D7, and bass inversions are notated using the forward slash symbol, D/A (D over A)
Functional chords are also notated in standard chord notation with tensions and slashed bass so as not to confuse tensions with inversions, except for the I64, Im64, the Neapolitan 6th (N6) and the German augmented sixth (Ger+6). For example: IVMaj7 (for the major 7th), IV/3 (for IV chord over the 3rd of the chord, or first inversion), or Im/b3 (for the Im in first inversion.)

Classical functional notation (such as i for Im or, I42 for I in third inversion) has not been used in these workbooks to accommodate jazz and contemporary music chord notation for standard songs repertoire. Keep in mind that the main objective of these workbooks is to map/learn chord functions in every key.

Decoding the Circle of Fifths

Following is a brief explanation of the **"Decoding the Circle of Fifths"** system.
Consider the standard circle of fifths:

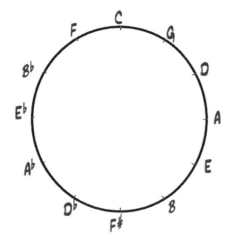

In this circle, **C** is the top node (note) and the rest of the nodes follow clockwise in intervals of perfect fifths.

We will label it as the *C circle of fifths by note* or the *circle of fifths in the key of C* (in any mode)

The letters in this circle represent notes only, not triads.

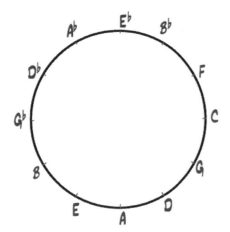

In this circle, **Eb** is the top node and the rest of the nodes follow clockwise in intervals of perfect fifths.

We will label this circle as the *Eb circle of fifths* or the *circle of fifths by note* in the key of Eb (in any mode)

The letters in this circle represent notes only, not triads.

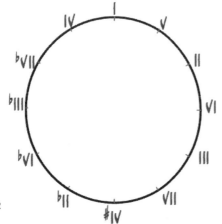

In this circle, **I** is the top node and the rest of the nodes follow clockwise in intervals of perfect fifths.

This is a relative or functional circle showing degrees only. Roman Numerals represent the intervals between each node and the top node.

We will consider this circle as a **functional circle of fifths**. The roman numerals in this circle represent degrees only (or mode free) since numerals do not show their triadic (or seventh) content type.

To graph a structure using the circle, join the nodes (notes) that belong to that structure. The following picture shows a functional graph of the major and minor scale, one for the harmonic scale, and one for the melodic minor. The arrows in the harmonic and melodic minor show the transformation made from the natural minor into these two *artificial* modes.

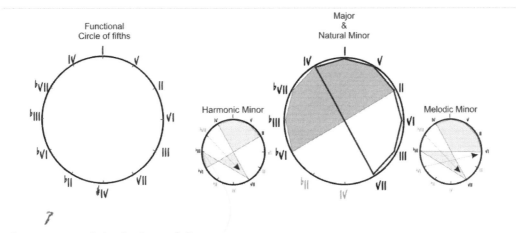

The same graph in the key of C:

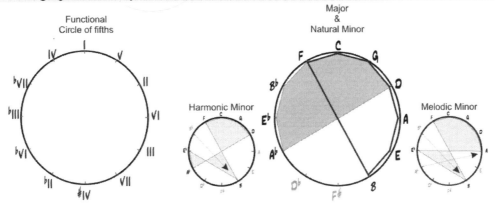

and in the key of Eb:

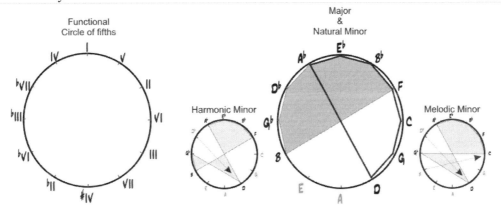

Note: *The arrows in the minor modes show how the Natural Minor was transformed into the Harmonic and Minor modes.*

Functional Circles using Triads and Seventh Chords

The two images in the this page show the same circle of fifths, now considering the triadic content and the seventh chords, for both the major mode and the minor complex (compound) mode.
Only the most often used chord functions are displayed in the minor mode.

Functional Circles using Triads

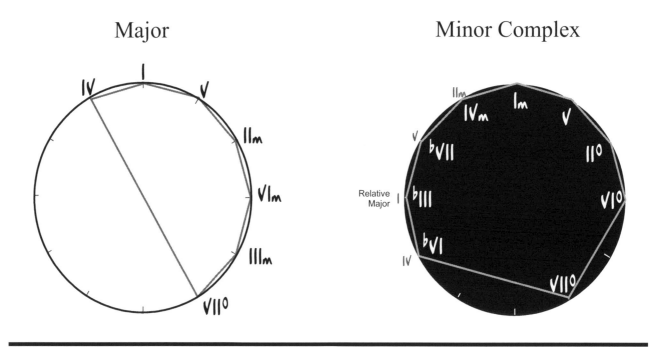

Functional Circles using Sevenths

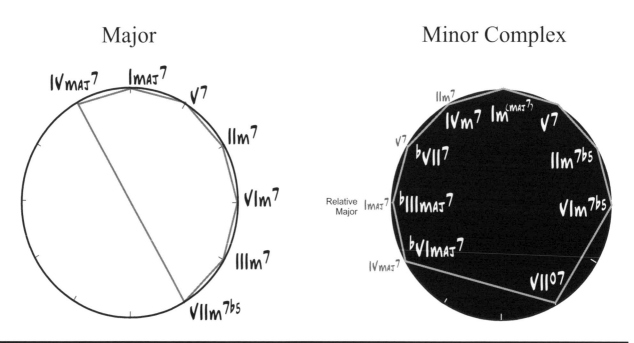

As an exercise, you may re-write these circles in the keys of C and Eb, and other keys as well.

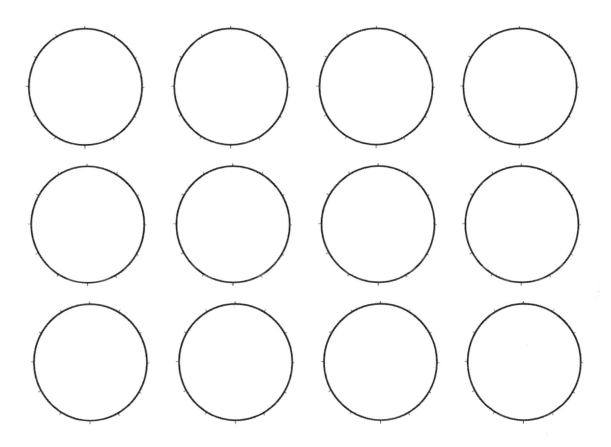

The circle of fifths is actually a primitive version of a tonal map. It successfully assigns a specific location for every diatonic function, in a logical and consistent manner based on essential harmonic principles, while predicting the most probable path for the roots of chord functions counterclockwise around the circle, leading to the I. On the other hand, it lacks clarity in classifying these functions by tension, at least in direct arrangement, since the three main regions: Tonic, Sub-Dominant & Dominant, are not clearly delimited or established.

Landscaping and Subjective Considerations

A final and definite version for our tonal harmony map will not be obtained by evolving/transforming the circle of fifths into a more complex graph that would clearly classify functions by tension, but by creating a landscape for the three main harmonic (tonic, sub-dominant, dominant) instead. Once a user-friendly landscape version for our map has been established, we will use the circle of fifths properties to assign a specific location for each harmonic function in said landscape.

The following page shows an outline of the map's main landscape and the standard or expected path for harmonic progressions in a tonal harmony context.

The landscape is divided into three regions:

Tonic	Sub-Dominant	Dominant
Home	Mountain	Ship in a Rough Sea

The representation for each region is purely subjective, based on the author's perception, and could be reinterpreted as a set of any other entities without affecting the functionality of the map.

The **Tonic** is located at the center and is our **Home**. (since it will be our point of departure, rest, and return, and it is the most stable region)

The **Sub-Dominant** is at the top left corner of the map, represented by a **Mountain** (since the historic use of the plagal cadence IV-I as in an *amen* ending, and the progression I-bVI, are usually perceived as a shift in the harmonic plane)

The **Dominant** is at the top right corner, represented by a **Ship in a Rough Sea** (the most unstable and tense region)

An arrow shows the standard path followed by harmonic progressions in a tonal context.
It is important to notice that a map based on this landscape can only represent one and only one key center at a time.

Tonal Harmony Landscape
&
Standard path for harmonic progressions

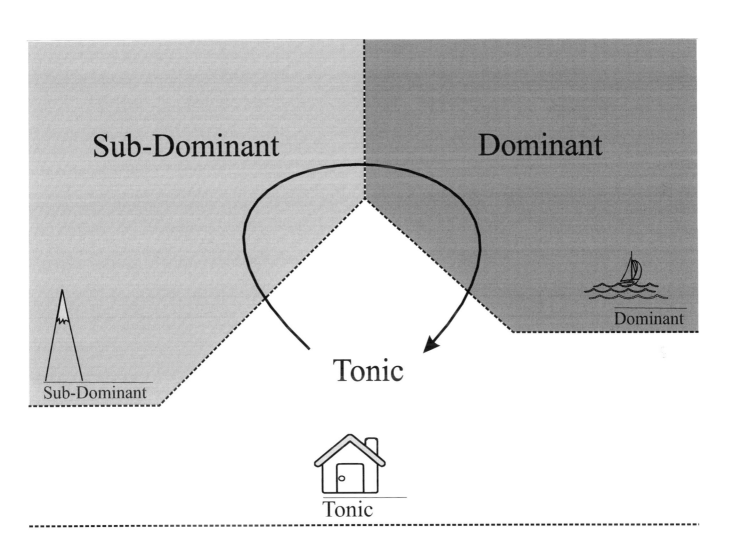

Mapping Diatonic Functions into the Landscape

Now that a landscape has been delineated, an analysis of the tension for each node in the circle of fifths will determine the location for each diatonic harmonic function.

Carefully study the diagram in the following page, where every function in the circle of fifths (major and minor) has been labeled with their respective harmonic region.

The diagram shows the process used to assign each function to a specific location in the landscape, as follows:

1) Each region contains a partial circle of fifths in the current key for the map.
2) Each harmonic function was assigned to the region it belongs, preserving its node's position in the original circle of fifth.
   I is assigned to the top node of the tonic circle. V7 is assigned to the "one o'clock" node of the dominant circle. IV is assigned to the "eleven o'clock" node of the sub-dominant circle.
3) Functions from the minor mode are in the inner part of the circle while functions from the major mode are in the outer part of the circle.

It is not surprising that the tension pattern counterclockwise is SD-D-T (subdominant, dominant, tonic) throughout all the diatonic functions with some exceptions.

Mapping Exceptions

Major: The exception in major is the IIIm. Following the tension pattern, IIIm should be a sub-dominant function. This is not true at all. As seen previously, IIIm contains the 7th which makes it a dominant chord, but it also contains the 3rd and 5th (the two most stable degrees after the 1st) which makes it a tonic chord. IIIm is an ambiguous chord and can't be assigned to any region specifically therefore, it will be located in a *limbo* between the Tonic and the Dominant. IIIm's functional region will have to be determined based on context.

Minor: The minor mode exception is the bVII7. By following the tension pattern over the circle of fifths it should be a dominant chord but, as mentioned earlier, it contains no 7th and a b6 which makes it a sub-dominant chord. Although the bVII7 should probably be assigned to the sub-dominant (because of its sound quality) it is common practice and simplicity in mapping that will decide its final location to the dominant region. As shown in the circle of fifths for the minor keys, the bVII7, not only should be labeled as a dominant (by following the tension pattern) but is also the V7 of the bIII (bIII is the relative major for the circle's tonic). In minor pieces, it is common practice to find harmonic progressions that lead to that bIII (relative major) using the bVII7 as its secondary dominant and also to deceptively resolve that bVII to the Im (instead of the bIII). Also the progression bVI-bVII-I (major) is often used in a major key when borrowing chords from the minor mode. The bVII is more often used as a cadential chord substituting a dominant function than as a sub-dominant one. Another very important point is that the final solution with the bVII in the dominant region, contains three minor and two major functions in each and every region.

Mapping Tonic, Sub-Dominant and Dominant

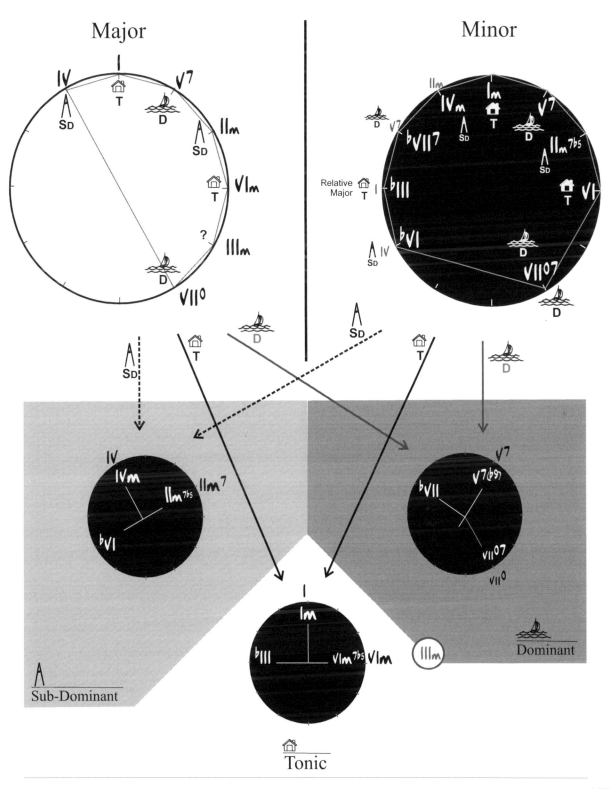

Major

Minor

Sub-Dominant

Dominant

Tonic

Scope of the workbooks

The volumes in this collection are organized in a progressive manner, each volume expanding the previous volume's map by introducing new harmonic concepts and/or functions, based on the premise that all functions introduced in earlier volumes have been understood and assimilated. Each new concept or function adds some level of detail to the map and/or extends the known area around the tonic.

Many of the concepts presented in these books are simply mentioned for mapping purposes only, and should be carefully studied by using other sources such as: a harmony course, tonal harmony books, teachers, etc.

Voice-leading and inversions are not covered in these volumes since their main objective is to map essential harmonic functions in every key.

Contents by Volume

Vol. 1
The basic major & minor diatonic neighborhoods
Tonic - Sub-Dominant - Dominant. Basic harmonic progressions.
- Perfect Authentic Cadence (PAC).
- The use of V7 vs. V as a triad.
- Standard/Basic Harmonic Progressions in the nearby diatonic neighborhood.
- Use of the Tonic- Subdominant - Dominant - Tonic progressions.
- Progression over the Circle of Fifths: vi-ii-V-I
- Substitution: IVMaj7 in place of IIm7 (subdominants)

Vol. 2
Mapping IIIm , I64, V7sus4 and deceptive cadences
The complete diatonic neighborhood for Major-Minor (borrowing from minor)
- Deceptive and Plagal Cadences.
- The IIIm (ambiguous chord : Tonic vs. Dominant).
- Cadential I64 or I/5, Im64 or Im/5 and the V7sus4: all preceding the V7.
- Borrowing chords from other modes (minor - major).

Vol. 3
More harmonic progressions and cadences in the diatonic neighborhood
Mapping the SubV7 and its use as a Neapolitan chord
- Inverted bass and bass lines. Pedal points: Tonic Pedal and Dominant Pedal.
- Backward progressions and other progressions outside the circle of fifths.
- The half cadence to V7 without secondary dominants.
- The Neapolitan Sixth Chord (bII/3 or N6) and the SubV7 (bII7).

Vol. 4
Basic Secondary dominants and their related IIm7
V7/x, viio7/x, IIm7/x
- Basic Secondary functions.
- Creating a temporary key center in the diatonic neighborhood.
- Secondary Dominants (V7 and VIIo7 and the related IIm7).
- Extended Dominants.

Vol. 5
Mapping blues I7 IV7. Additional minor mode functions
The bIIMaj7 subdominant minor and its related IIm7-V7

- More borrowed chords from other modes and paths to modulations.
- The IV7 from dorian minor.
- The modal Vm.
- The bIIMaj7 subdominant minor chord (or root-altered IIm7b5) and its related IIm7 and V7. The I7 as tonic in the Blues and Blues form.

Vol. 6
Advanced secondary functions and deceptive secondary cadences
Secondary cadential I64s & V7sus. Mapping IV/x , bVI/x, bVII7/x, viio7/x

- Other Secondary functions: IV/x bVI/x and bVII/x
- Creating a temporary Tonic in the diatonic neighborhood using secondary IV/x, bVI/x and bVII/x.
- More borrowing from other modes and paths to modulations.
- Secondary cadential 64s & V7sus.

Vol. 7
The entire MAP, including all secondary functions
Mapping all secondary subVs/x and their related IIm. The N6 and Gr+6

- More Secondary functions: SubV7/X .
- The Neapolitan 6 N6/X (same as SubV/3 no 7)
- The Augmented 6th chords. Gr+6, It+6, Fr+6.
- The related IIm7/X for the SubV7/X.
- Extended dominants. Reinterpreting chord functions. New paths to modulations.

Worksheets

in all keys

Study/locate the new functions on the map
Write/play suggested progressions for the current key
Write your own progressions in the composer's log
Complete the fill-in-the-blanks map

Example
In the key of **I**

Mapping blues I7 IV7. Additional minor mode functions.
The bIImaj7 subdominant minor and its related IIm7-V7

New Chords/Functions in the current level

Tonic: I⁷ Blues Tonic

Sub-Dominant: IV⁷ ♭II and ♭IImaj⁷

Dominant: Vm modal Vm

Secondary: IIm⁷ and V⁷ of ♭IImaj⁷

Harmonic Progressions examples

I⁷	IV⁷	I⁷	I⁷	IV⁷	VII°⁷ of V
I/⁵	V⁷	IIm⁷	V⁷	I⁷ V⁷ of II	V⁷ of V V⁷
Im	IV⁷	Im	IV⁷	♭III	IV
Im	IV⁷	♭III	IV	Im	Im
Im	(IIm⁷ V⁷) of ♭II	♭IImaj⁷	IIm⁷♭⁵	V⁷	Im
Im	(IIm⁷ V⁷) of ♭II	♭IImaj⁷	V⁷	Im ♭IImaj⁷	I
I	Vm	I	Vm	I Vm	I
Im	Vm	Im	Vm	Im Vm	Im
I⁷	♭VII IV	I	IV⁷ ♭VII	I	♭VI ♭VII
I	IV⁷	I⁷	IV⁷	I	I⁷

Write down the same progressions in other keys using the map for the new key.

Concepts

More borrowed chords from other modes and paths to modulations.

The IV7 from dorian minor. The modal Vm.

The bIImaj7 subdominant minor chord (or root-altered IIm7b5) and its related
IIm7 and V7. The I7 as tonic in the Blues and Blues form.

Mapping blues I7 IV7. Additional minor mode functions.
The bIImaj7 subdominant minor and its related IIm7-V7

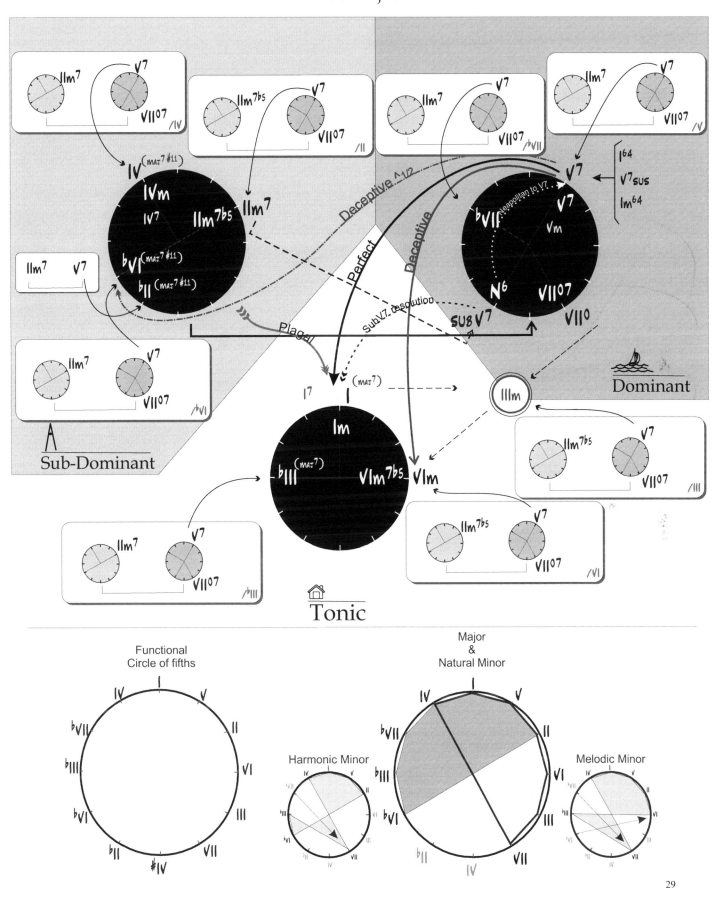

Functional
Circle of fifths

Major
&
Natural Minor

Harmonic Minor

Melodic Minor

Sub-Dominant

Tonic

Dominant

29

Mapping blues I7 IV7. Additional minor mode functions.
The bIImaj7 subdominant minor and its related IIm7-V7

New Chords/Functions in the current level

Tonic: C^7

Sub-Dominant: F^7 D^b AND D^bMAJ^7

Dominant: Gm MODAL Vm

Secondary: IIm^7 AND V^7 OF ^{b}IIMAJ^7

Harmonic Progressions examples

C^7	F^7	C^7	C^7	F^7	$F\sharp°7$
C/G	A^7	Dm^7	G^7	C^7 A^7	D^7 G^7
Cm	F^7	Cm	F^7	E^b	F
Cm	F^7	E^b	F	Cm	Cm
Cm	E^bm^7 $A^b{}^7$	D^bMAJ^7	Dm^{7b5}	G^7	Cm
Cm	E^bm^7 $A^b{}^7$	D^bMAJ^7	G^7	Cm D^bMAJ^7	C
C	Gm	C	Gm	C Gm	C
Cm	Gm	Cm	Gm	Cm Gm	Cm
C^7	B^b F	C	F^7 B^b	C	A^b B^b
C	F^7	C^7	F^7	C	C^7

Write down the same progressions in other keys using the map for the new key.

Concepts

More borrowed chords from other modes and paths to modulations.

The IV7 from dorian minor. The modal Vm.

The bIImaj7 subdominant minor chord (or root-altered IIm7b5) and its related
IIm7 and V7. The I7 as tonic in the Blues and Blues form.

Key of C

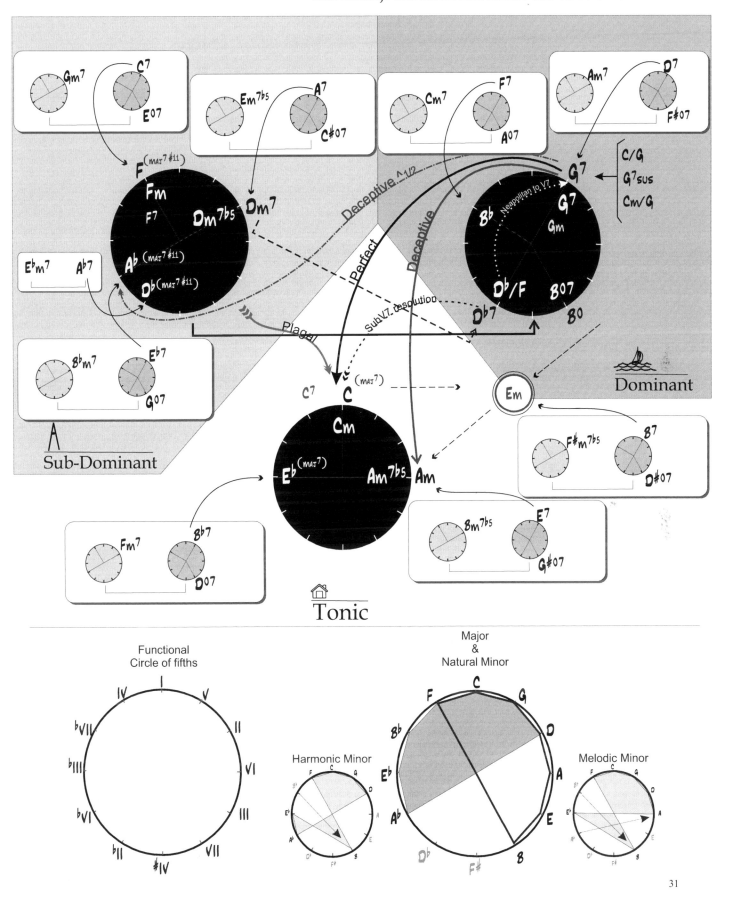

Composer's Diary

Compose your own harmonic progressions in the current key.
Include the new chords/functions introduced in this chapter.

Do not forget the clefs, key signature and meter

Key of C

Mapping blues I7 IV7. Additional minor mode functions.
The bIImaj7 subdominant minor and its related IIm7-V7

Complete the Map for the current key by filling in the blanks

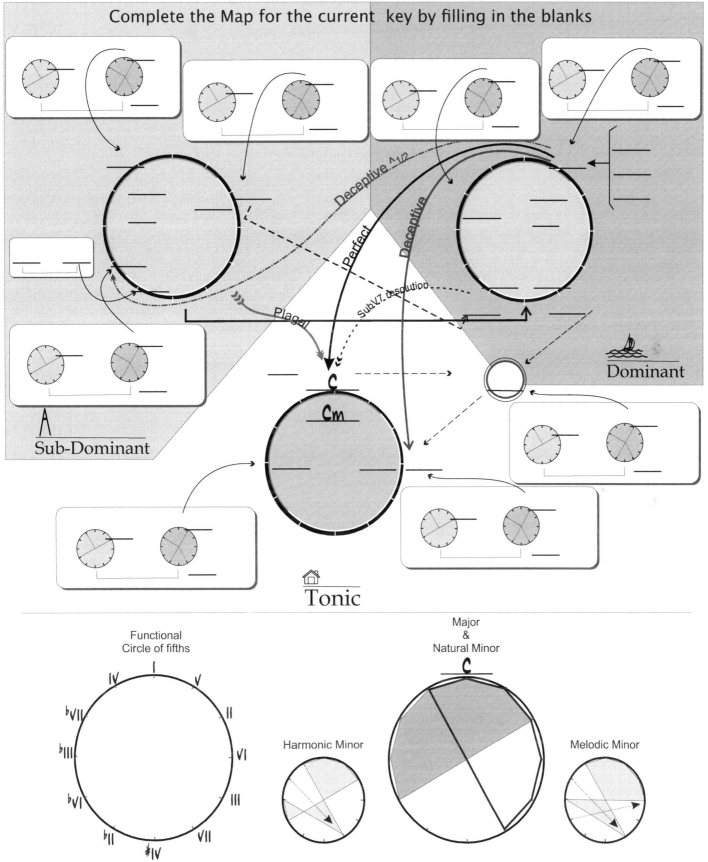

Sub-Dominant

Dominant

Tonic

Functional
Circle of fifths

Major
&
Natural Minor

Harmonic Minor

Melodic Minor

Functional Progressions   Worksheet

1

I^7	IV^7	I^7	I^7	IV^7	VII^{o7} of V
$I/^5$	V^7	IIm^7	V^7	I^7 V^7 of II	V^7 of V V^7

2

Im	IV^7	Im	IV^7	$^\flat III$	IV
Im	IV^7	$^\flat III$	IV	Im	Im

3

Im	$^\angle IIm^7$ V^7 of $^\flat II$	$^\flat II\,maj^7$	$IIm^{7\flat 5}$	V^7	Im
Im	$^\angle IIm^7$ V^7 of $^\flat II$	$^\flat II\,maj^7$	V^7	Im $^\flat II\,maj^7$	I

4

I	Vm	I	Vm	I Vm	I
Im	Vm	Im	Vm	Im Vm	Im

5

I^7	$^\flat VII$ IV	I	IV^7 $^\flat VII$	I	$^\flat VI$ $^\flat VII$
I	IV^7	I^7	IV^7	I	I^7

Write down the same progressions in the current key and play them.

1
2
3
4
5

34

Key of C#

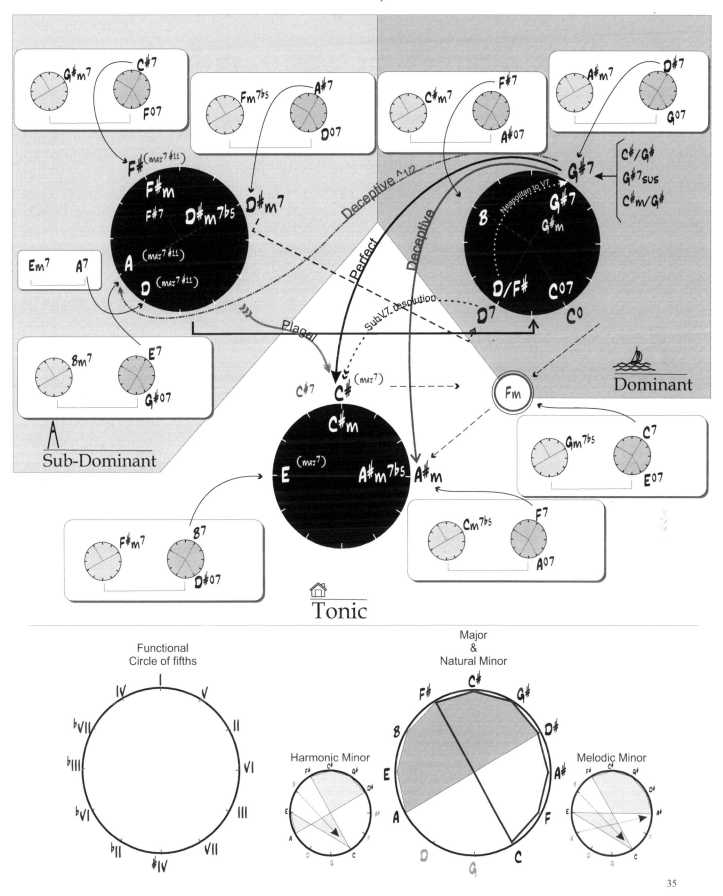

Composer's Diary

Compose your own harmonic progressions in the current key.
Include the new chords/functions introduced in this chapter.

Do not forget the clefs, key signature and meter

Key of C♯

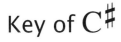

Mapping blues I7 IV7. Additional minor mode functions.
The bIImaj7 subdominant minor and its related IIm7-V7

Complete the Map for the current key by filling in the blanks

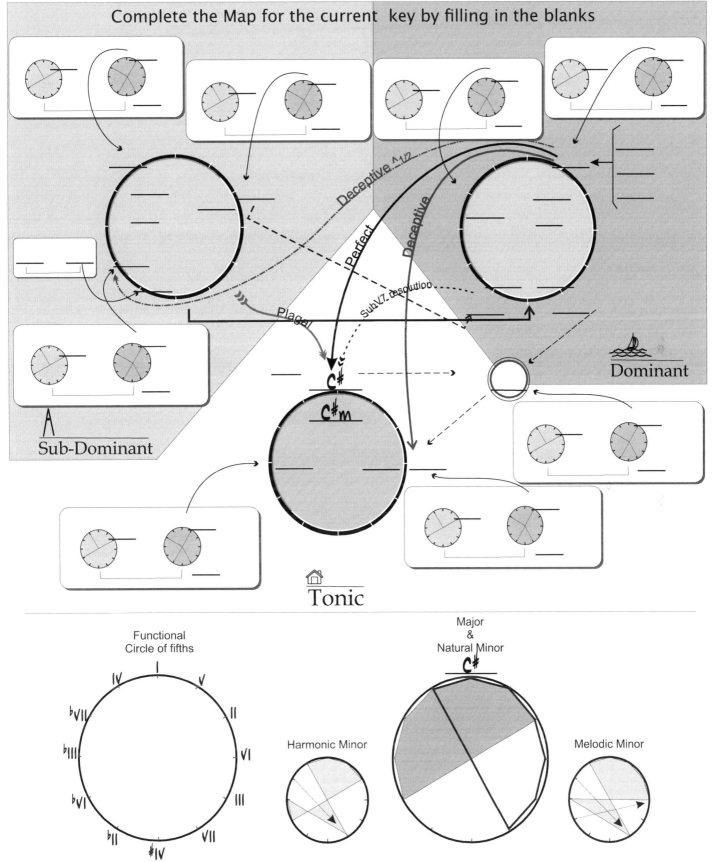

Sub-Dominant

Dominant

Tonic

C♯

C♯m

A

Deceptive ^1/2

Deceptive

Perfect

Plagal

SubV7 resolution

Functional
Circle of fifths

Major
&
Natural Minor

C♯

Harmonic Minor

Melodic Minor

IV   I   V

bVII   II

bIII   VI

bVI   III

bII   VII

♯IV

37

Example
In the key of D♭

Mapping blues I7 IV7. Additional minor mode functions.
The bIImaj7 subdominant minor and its related IIm7-V7

New Chords/Functions in the current level

Tonic: $D♭7$

Sub-Dominant: $G♭7$ D   AND   D maj7

Dominant: $A♭m$ MODAL Vm

Secondary: IIm7 AND V7 OF ♭IImaj7

Harmonic Progressions examples

D♭7	G♭7	D♭7	D♭7	G♭7	G°7
D♭/A♭	B♭7	E♭m7	A♭7	D♭7 B♭7	E♭7 A♭7
D♭m	G♭7	D♭m	G♭7	E	G♭
D♭m	G♭7	E	G♭	D♭m	D♭m
D♭m	Em7 A7	D maj7	E♭m7♭5	A♭7	D♭m
D♭m	Em7 A7	D maj7	A♭7	D♭m D maj7	D♭
D♭	A♭m	D♭	A♭m	D♭ A♭m	D♭
D♭m	A♭m	D♭m	A♭m	D♭m A♭m	D♭m
D♭7	B G♭	D♭	G♭7 B	D♭	A B
D♭	G♭7	D♭7	G♭7	D♭	D♭7

Write down the same progressions in other keys using the map for the new key.

Concepts

More borrowed chords from other modes and paths to modulations.

The IV7 from dorian minor. The modal Vm.

The bIImaj7 subdominant minor chord (or root-altered IIm7b5) and its related

IIm7 and V7. The I7 as tonic in the Blues and Blues form.

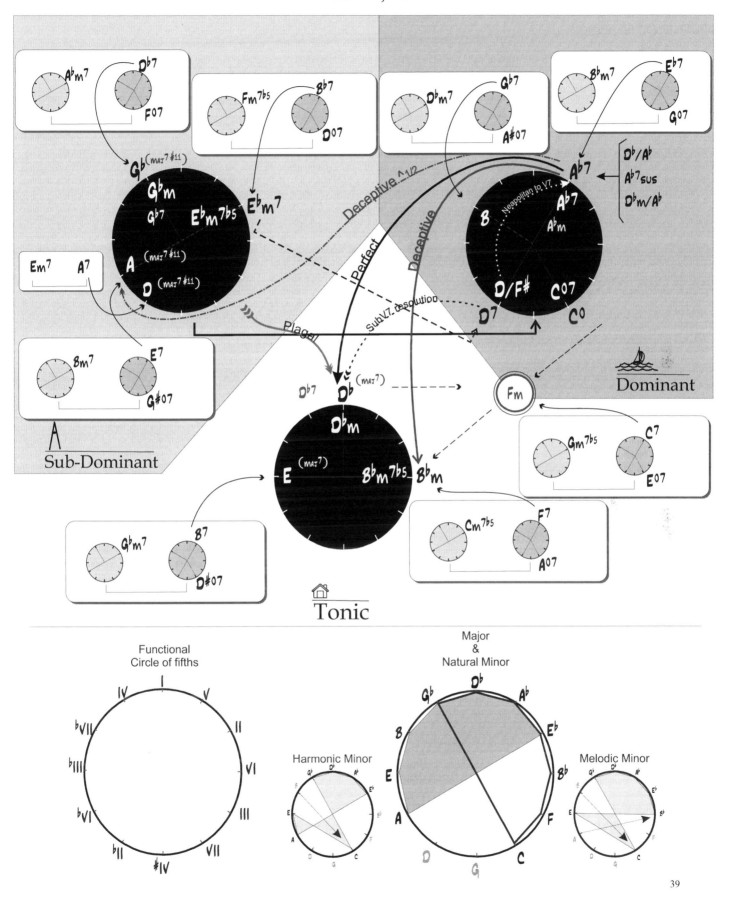

Composer's Diary

Compose your own harmonic progressions in the current key.
Include the new chords/functions introduced in this chapter.

Do not forget the clefs, key signature and meter

Key of D♭

Mapping blues I7 IV7. Additional minor mode functions.
The bIImaj7 subdominant minor and its related IIm7-V7

Complete the Map for the current key by filling in the blanks

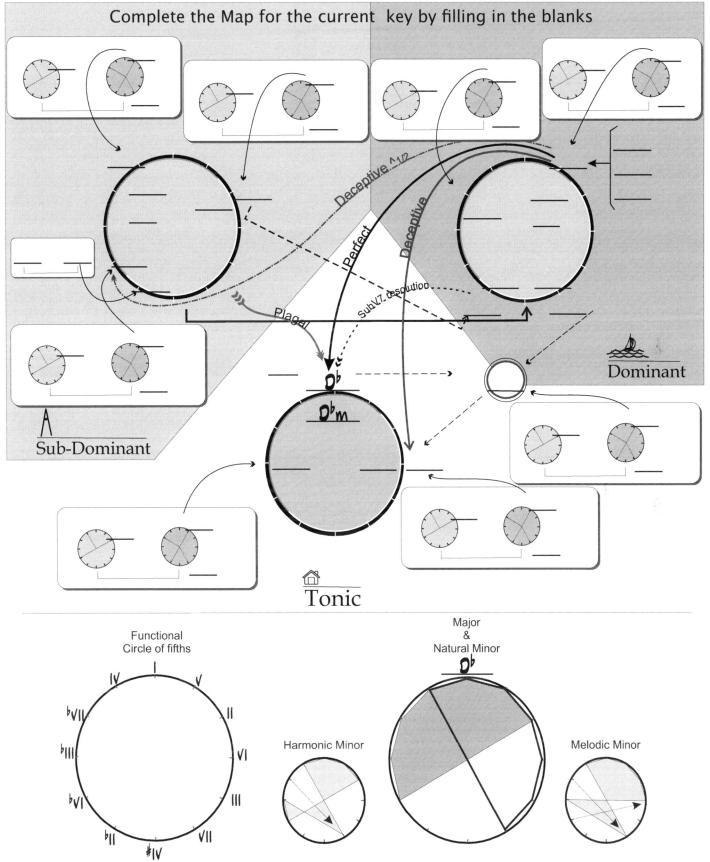

Deceptive ^1/2

Deceptive

Perfect

SubV7 resolution

Plagal

Dominant

Sub-Dominant

D♭

D♭m

Tonic

Functional
Circle of fifths

Major
&
Natural Minor

D♭

Harmonic Minor

Melodic Minor

I
IV
V
II
bVII
bIII
VI
bVI
III
bII
VII
#IV

Functional Progressions — Worksheet

1	I^7	IV^7	I^7	I^7	IV^7	VII^{o7} of V
	$I/^5$	V^7	IIm^7	V^7	I^7 V^7 of II	V^7 of V V^7
2	Im	IV^7	Im	IV^7	♭III	IV
	Im	IV^7	♭III	IV	Im	Im
3	Im	(IIm^7 V^7) of ♭II	♭II maj^7	IIm^{7b5}	V^7	Im
	Im	(IIm^7 V^7) of ♭II	♭II maj^7	V^7	Im ♭II maj^7	I
4	I	Vm	I	Vm	I Vm	I
	Im	Vm	Im	Vm	Im Vm	Im
5	I^7	♭VII IV	I	IV^7 ♭VII	I	♭VI ♭VII
	I	IV^7	I^7	IV^7	I	I^7

Write down the same progressions in the current key and play them.

1						
2						
3						
4						
5						

Key of D

Mapping blues I7 IV7. Additional minor mode functions.
The bIImaj7 subdominant minor and its related IIm7-V7

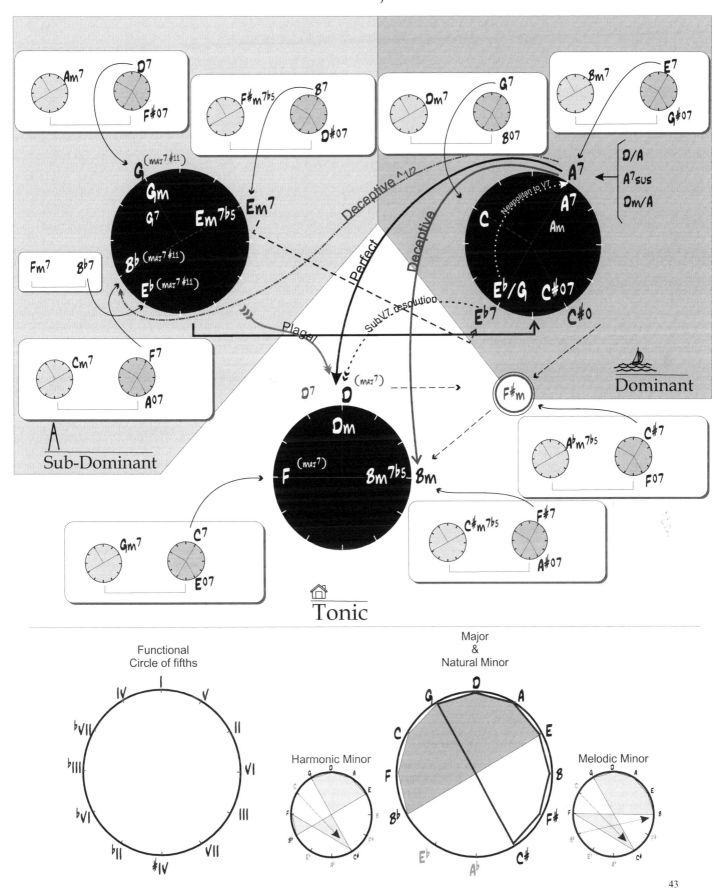

Composer's Diary

Compose your own harmonic progressions in the current key.
Include the new chords/functions introduced in this chapter.

Do not forget the clefs, key signature and meter

Key of D

Mapping blues I7 IV7. Additional minor mode functions.
The bIImaj7 subdominant minor and its related IIm7-V7

Complete the Map for the current key by filling in the blanks

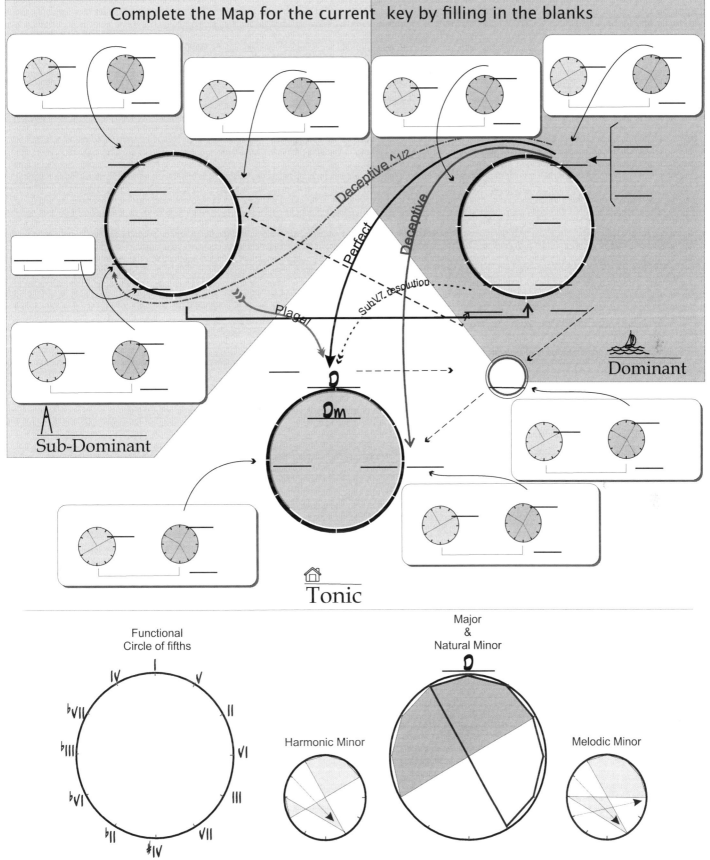

Deceptive ^1/2

Deceptive

Perfect

SubV7 resolution

Plagal

Dm

D

Dominant

A
Sub-Dominant

Tonic

Functional
Circle of fifths

I
IV   V
bVII   II
bIII   VI
bVI   III
bII   VII
#IV

Major
&
Natural Minor

D

Harmonic Minor

Melodic Minor

45

Functional Progressions
Worksheet

1

I^7	IV^7	I^7	I^7	IV^7	VII^{o7} OF V
$I/5$	V^7	IIm^7	V^7	I^7 V^7 OF II	V^7 OF V V^7

2

Im	IV^7	Im	IV^7	$^\flat III$	IV
Im	IV^7	$^\flat III$	IV	Im	Im

3

Im	$(IIm^7$ $V^7)$ OF $^\flat II$	$^\flat II$ MAJ^7	$IIm^{7\flat5}$	V^7	Im
Im	$(IIm^7$ $V^7)$ OF $^\flat II$	$^\flat II$ MAJ^7	V^7	Im $^\flat II$ MAJ^7	I

4

I	Vm	I	Vm	I Vm	I
Im	Vm	Im	Vm	Im Vm	Im

5

I^7	$^\flat VII$ IV	I	IV^7 $^\flat VII$	I	$^\flat VI$ $^\flat VII$
I	IV^7	I^7	IV^7	I	I^7

Write down the same progressions in the current key and play them.

1

2

3

4

5

46

Key of D♯

Mapping blues I7 IV7. Additional minor mode functions.
The bIImaj7 subdominant minor and its related IIm7-V7

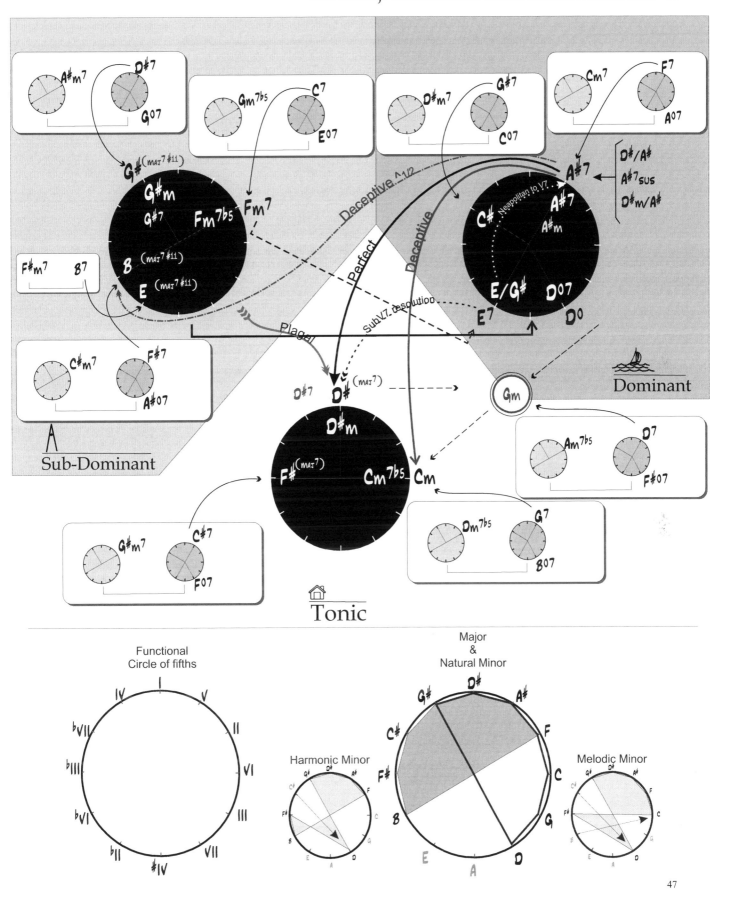

Composer's Diary

Compose your own harmonic progressions in the current key.
Include the new chords/functions introduced in this chapter.

Do not forget the clefs, key signature and meter

Key of D♯

Complete the Map for the current key by filling in the blanks

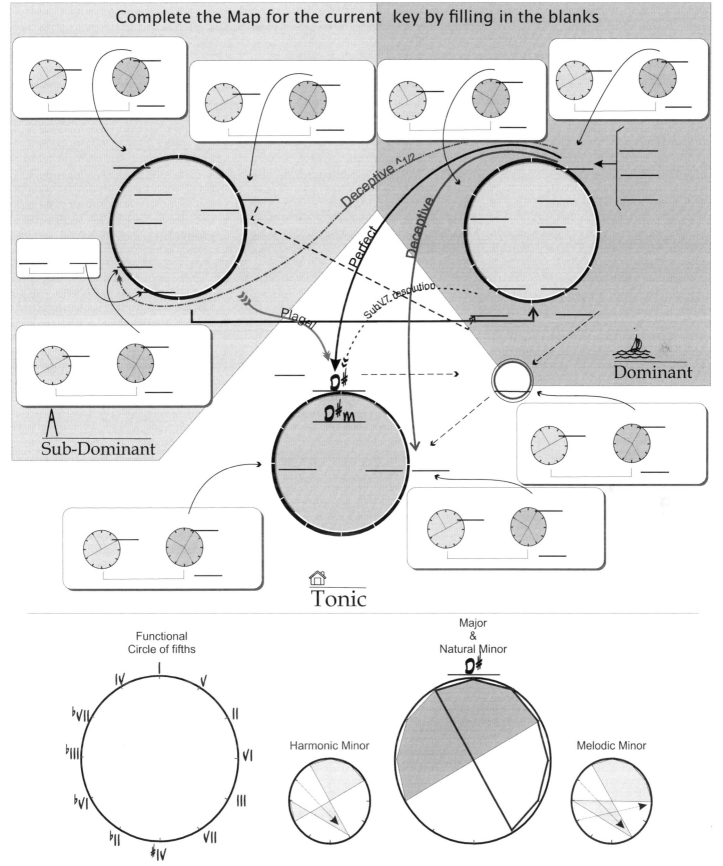

Deceptive ^1/2

Deceptive

Perfect

SubV7 resolution

Plagal

Dominant

A
Sub-Dominant

🏠
Tonic

D♯

D♯m

Functional
Circle of fifths

I
IV
V
II
VI
III
VII
#IV
bII
bVI
bIII
bVII

Major
&
Natural Minor
D♯

Harmonic Minor

Melodic Minor

1

I^7	IV^7	I^7	I^7	IV^7	$VII°^7$ of V
$I/5$	V^7	IIm^7	V^7	I^7 V^7 of II	V^7 of V V^7

2

Im	IV^7	Im	IV^7	$♭III$	IV
Im	IV^7	$♭III$	IV	Im	Im

3

Im	$(IIm^7 \; V^7)$ of $♭II$	$♭II\,maj^7$	$IIm^{7♭5}$	V^7	Im
Im	$(IIm^7 \; V^7)$ of $♭II$	$♭II\,maj^7$	V^7	Im $♭II\,maj^7$	I

4

I	Vm	I	Vm	I Vm	I
Im	Vm	Im	Vm	Im Vm	Im

5

I^7	$♭VII$ IV	I	IV^7 $♭VII$	I	$♭VI$ $♭VII$
I	IV^7	I^7	IV^7	I	I^7

Write down the same progressions in the current key and play them.

1

2

3

4

5

Key of E♭

Mapping blues I7 IV7. Additional minor mode functions.
The bIImaj7 subdominant minor and its related IIm7-V7

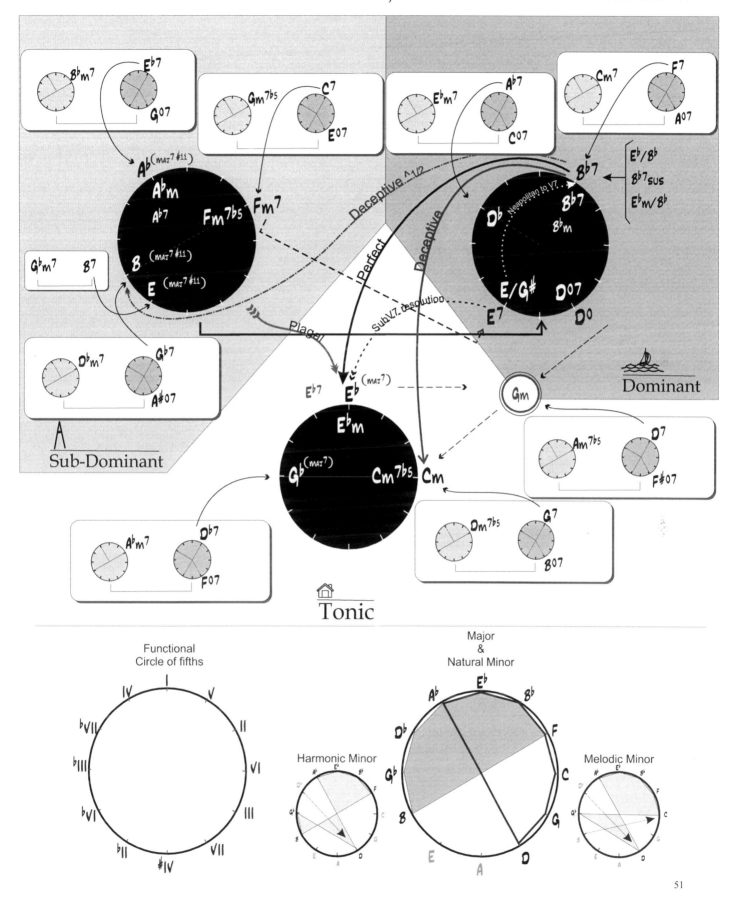

Sub-Dominant

Tonic

Dominant

Functional
Circle of fifths

Major
&
Natural Minor

Harmonic Minor

Melodic Minor

Composer's Diary

Compose your own harmonic progressions in the current key.
Include the new chords/functions introduced in this chapter.

Do not forget the clefs, key signature and meter

Key of E♭

Mapping blues I7 IV7. Additional minor mode functions.
The bIImaj7 subdominant minor and its related IIm7-V7

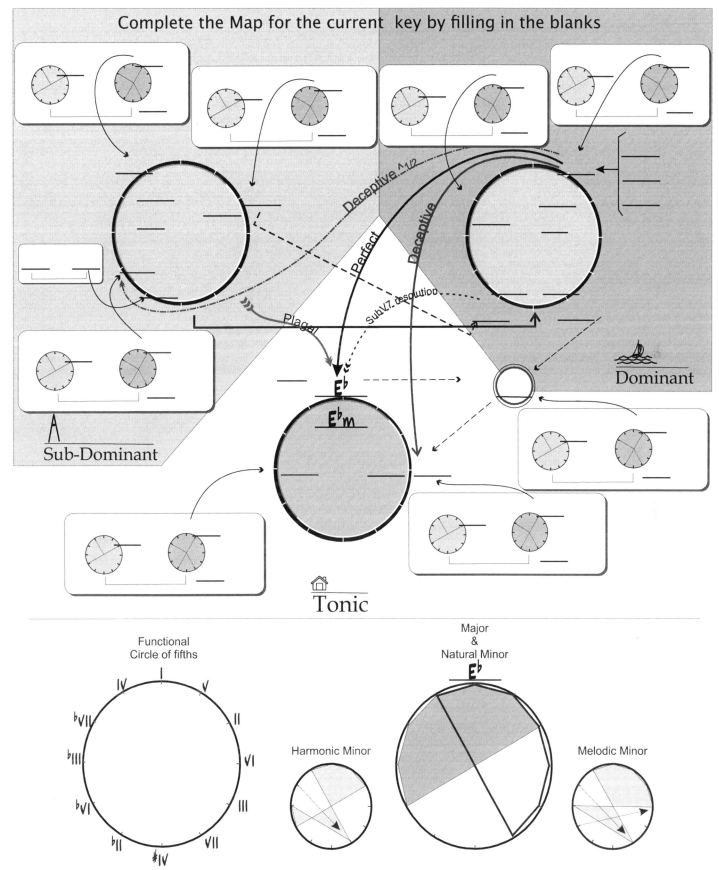

Complete the Map for the current key by filling in the blanks

Sub-Dominant

Dominant

Tonic

Functional Circle of fifths

Major & Natural Minor

Harmonic Minor

Melodic Minor

Functional Progressions — Worksheet

1

I⁷	IV⁷	I⁷	I⁷	IV⁷	VII°⁷ ᴏꜰ V
I/⁵	V⁷	IIm⁷	V⁷	I⁷ V⁷ ᴏꜰ II	V⁷ ᴏꜰ V V⁷

2

Im	IV⁷	Im	IV⁷	♭III	IV
Im	IV⁷	♭III	IV	Im	Im

3

Im	♭IIm⁷ V⁷ ᴏꜰ ♭II	♭II ᴍᴀᴊ⁷	IIm⁷♭⁵	V⁷	Im
Im	♭IIm⁷ V⁷ ᴏꜰ ♭II	♭II ᴍᴀᴊ⁷	V⁷	Im ♭II ᴍᴀᴊ⁷	I

4

I	Vm	I	Vm	I Vm	I
Im	Vm	Im	Vm	Im Vm	Im

5

I⁷	♭VII IV	I	IV⁷ ♭VII	I	♭VI ♭VII
I	IV⁷	I⁷	IV⁷	I	I⁷

Write down the same progressions in the current key and play them.

1

2

3

4

5

54

Key of E

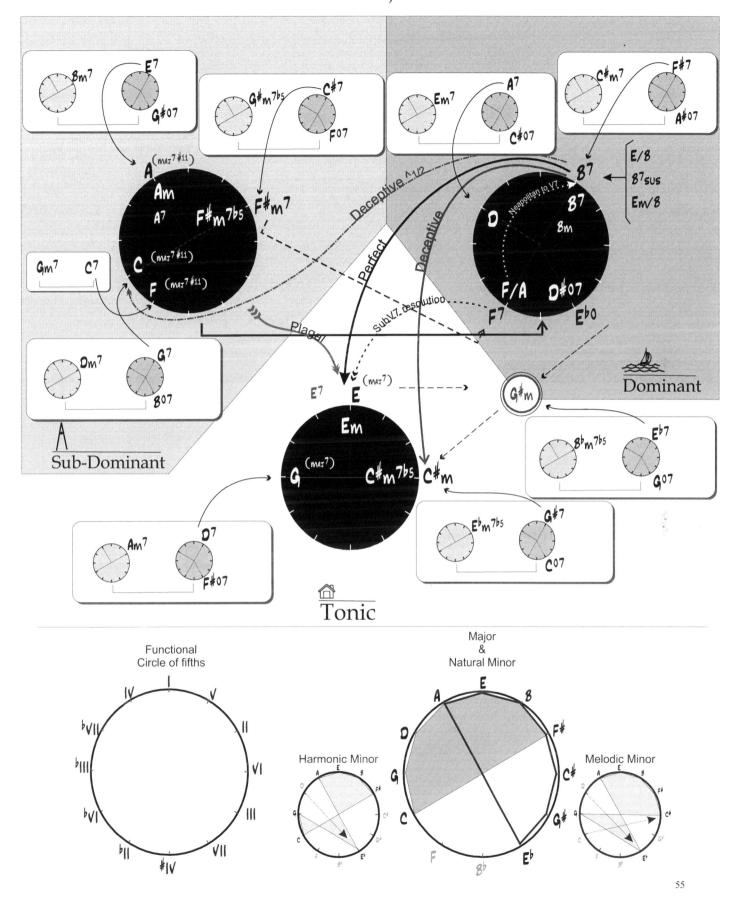

Composer's Diary

Compose your own harmonic progressions in the current key.
Include the new chords/functions introduced in this chapter.

Do not forget the clefs, key signature and meter

Key of E

Mapping blues I7 IV7. Additional minor mode functions.
The bIImaj7 subdominant minor and its related IIm7-V7

Complete the Map for the current key by filling in the blanks

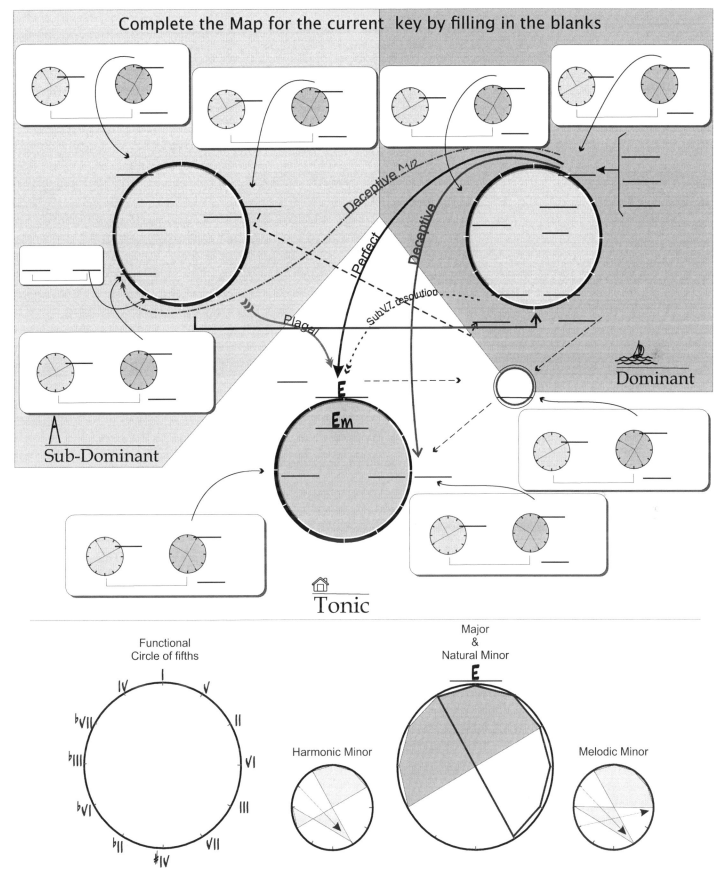

Deceptive ^1/2

Deceptive

Perfect

Plagal

SubV7 desolution

Dominant

Sub-Dominant

E

Em

Tonic

Functional
Circle of fifths

I

IV   V

bVII   II

bIII   VI

bVI   III

bII   VII

#IV

Major
&
Natural Minor

E

Harmonic Minor

Melodic Minor

Functional Progressions Worksheet

1					
I^7	IV^7	I^7	I^7	IV^7	VII^{o7} OF V
$I/5$	V^7	IIm^7	V^7	I^7 V^7 OF II	V^7 OF V V^7

2					
Im	IV^7	Im	IV^7	$\flat III$	IV
Im	IV^7	$\flat III$	IV	Im	Im

3					
Im	$(IIm^7$ $V^7)$ OF $\flat II$	$\flat II$ MAJ^7	$IIm^{7\flat5}$	V^7	Im
Im	$(IIm^7$ $V^7)$ OF $\flat II$	$\flat II$ MAJ^7	V^7	Im $\flat II$ MAJ^7	I

4					
I	Vm	I	Vm	I Vm	I
Im	Vm	Im	Vm	Im Vm	Im

5					
I^7	$\flat VII$ IV	I	IV^7 $\flat VII$	I	$\flat VI$ $\flat VII$
I	IV^7	I^7	IV^7	I	I^7

Write down the same progressions in the current key and play them.

1

2

3

4

5

58

Key of F

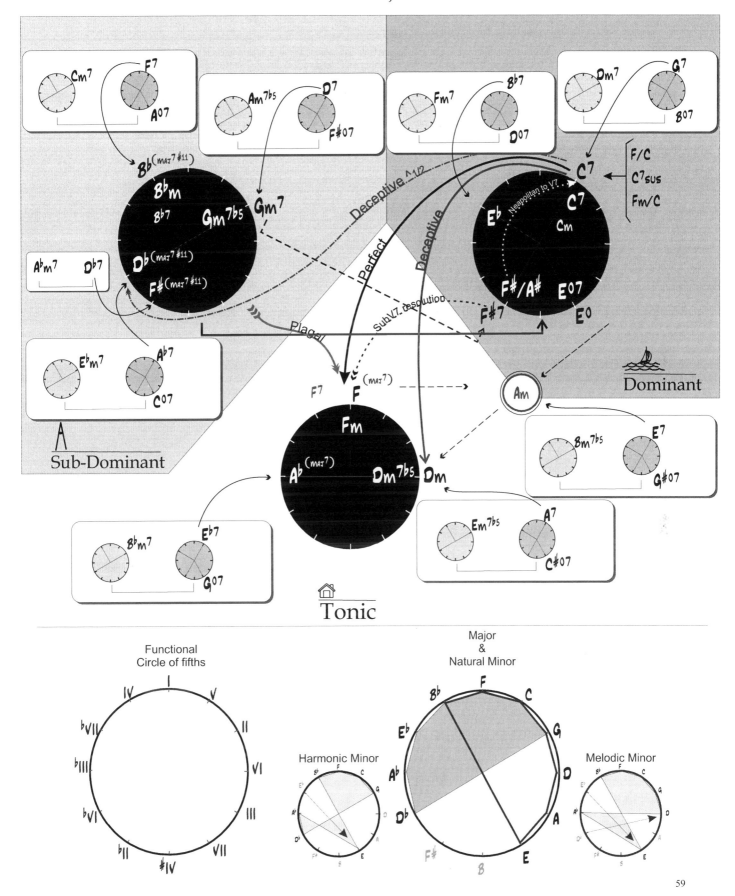

Composer's Diary

Compose your own harmonic progressions in the current key.
Include the new chords/functions introduced in this chapter.

Do not forget the clefs, key signature and meter

Key of F

Complete the Map for the current key by filling in the blanks

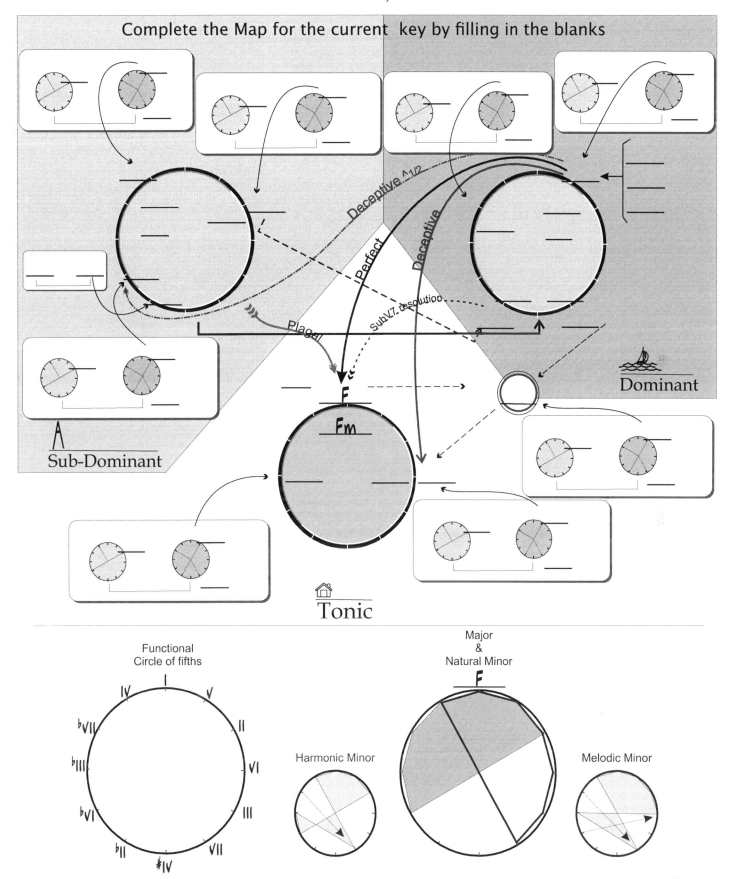

Deceptive ^1/2

Deceptive

Perfect

SubV7 resolution

Plagal

F

Fm

Dominant

A

Sub-Dominant

Tonic

Functional
Circle of fifths

IV   I   V

bVII   II

bIII   VI

bVI   III

bII   VII

#IV

Major
&
Natural Minor

F

Harmonic Minor

Melodic Minor

Example
In the key of F#

Mapping blues I7 IV7. Additional minor mode functions.
The bIImaj7 subdominant minor and its related IIm7-V7

New Chords/Functions in the current level

Tonic: F#7

Sub-Dominant: B7 G and Gmaj7

Dominant: C#m modal Vm

Secondary: IIm7 and V7 of bIImaj7

Harmonic Progressions examples

F#7	B7	F#7	F#7	B7	C°7
F#/C#	D#7	G#m7	C#7	F#7 D#7	G#7 C#7
F#m	B7	F#m	B7	A	B
F#m	B7	A	B	F#m	F#m
F#m	Am7 D7	Gmaj7	G#m7b5	C#7	F#m
F#m	Am7 D7	Gmaj7	C#7	F#m Gmaj7	F#
F#	C#m	F#	C#m	F# C#m	F#
F#m	C#m	F#m	C#m	F#m C#m	F#m
F#7	E B	F#	B7 E	F#	D E
F#	B7	F#7	B7	F#	F#7

Write down the same progressions in other keys using the map for the new key.

Concepts

More borrowed chords from other modes and paths to modulations.

The IV7 from dorian minor. The modal Vm.

The bIImaj7 subdominant minor chord (or root-altered IIm7b5) and its related IIm7 and V7. The I7 as tonic in the Blues and Blues form.

Key of F#

Mapping blues I7 IV7. Additional minor mode functions.
The bIImaj7 subdominant minor and its related IIm7-V7

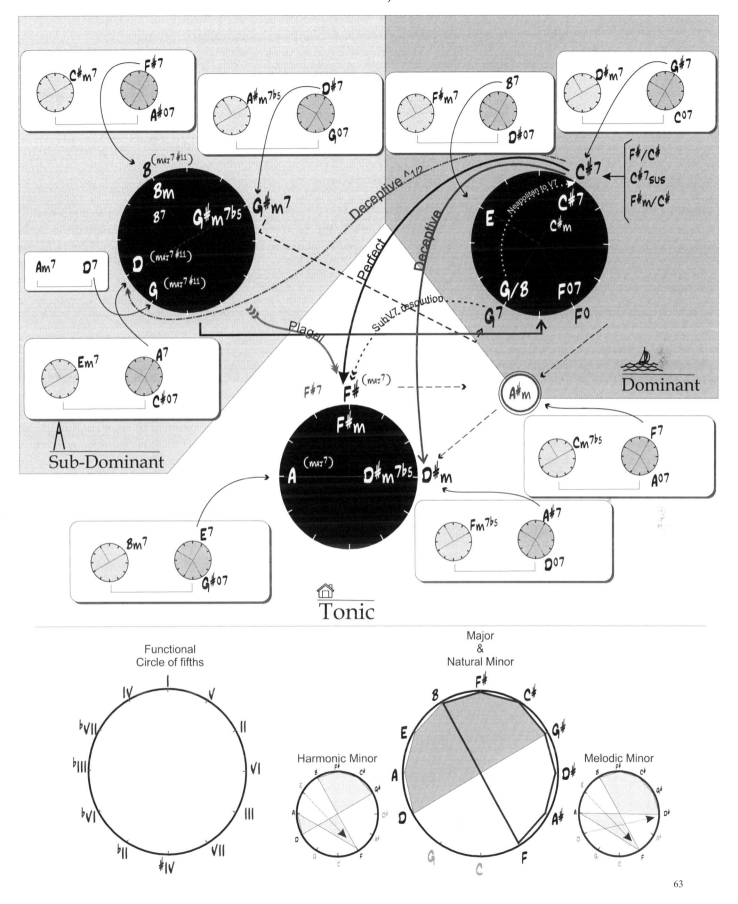

Composer's Diary

Compose your own harmonic progressions in the current key.
Include the new chords/functions introduced in this chapter.

Do not forget the clefs, key signature and meter

Key of F♯

Mapping blues I7 IV7. Additional minor mode functions.
The bIImaj7 subdominant minor and its related IIm7-V7

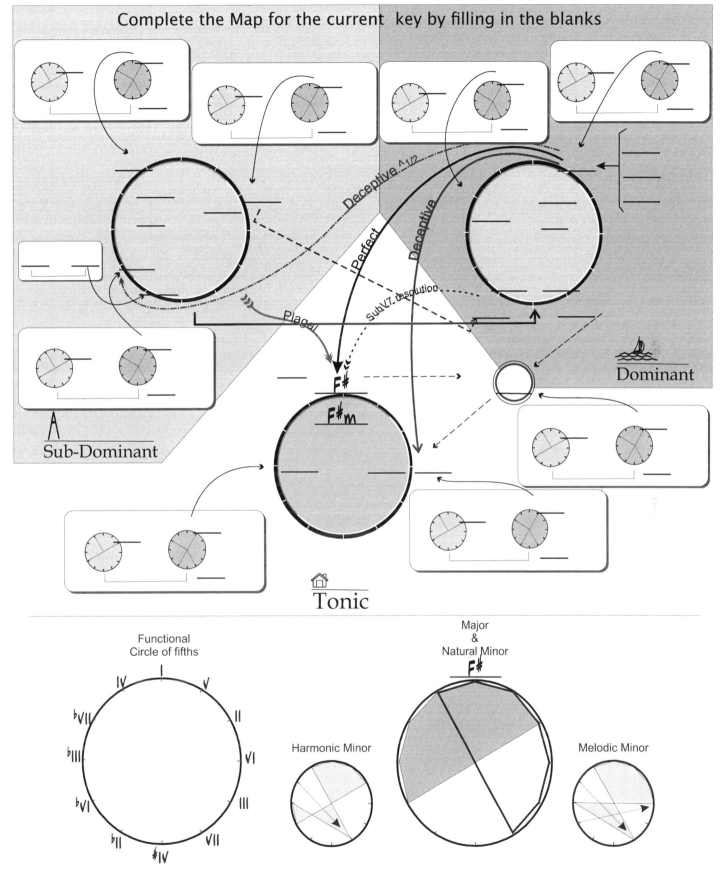

Complete the Map for the current key by filling in the blanks

A
Sub-Dominant

Deceptive ♭1/2

Deceptive

Perfect

SubV7 desolution

Plagal

F♯

F♯m

Dominant

🏠
Tonic

Functional
Circle of fifths

IV   I   V

♭VII   II

♭III   VI

♭VI   III

♭II   VII

♯IV

Major
&
Natural Minor

F♯

Harmonic Minor

Melodic Minor

Functional Progressions

1

I^7	IV^7	I^7	I^7	IV^7	VII^{07} of V
$I/^5$	V^7	IIm^7	V^7	I^7 V^7 of II	V^7 of V V^7

2

Im	IV^7	Im	IV^7	$♭III$	IV
Im	IV^7	$♭III$	IV	Im	Im

3

Im	$(IIm^7$ $V^7)$ of $♭II$	$♭II$ maj7	$IIm^{7♭5}$	V^7	Im
Im	$(IIm^7$ $V^7)$ of $♭II$	$♭II$ maj7	V^7	Im $♭II$ maj7	I

4

I	Vm	I	Vm	I Vm	I
Im	Vm	Im	Vm	Im Vm	Im

5

I^7	$♭VII$ IV	I	IV^7 $♭VII$	I	$♭VI$ $♭VII$
I	IV^7	I^7	IV^7	I	I^7

Write down the same progressions in the current key and play them.

1

2

3

4

5

Key of G♭

Mapping blues I7 IV7. Additional minor mode functions.
The bIImaj7 subdominant minor and its related IIm7-V7

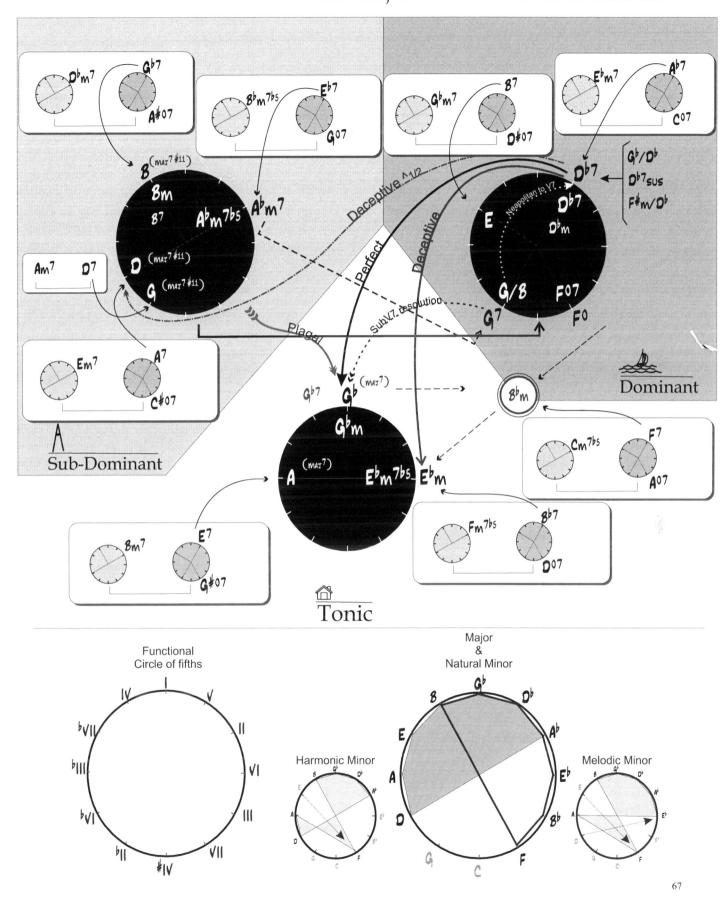

Composer's Diary

Compose your own harmonic progressions in the current key.
Include the new chords/functions introduced in this chapter.

Do not forget the clefs, key signature and meter

Key of G♭

Mapping blues I7 IV7. Additional minor mode functions.
The bIImaj7 subdominant minor and its related IIm7-V7

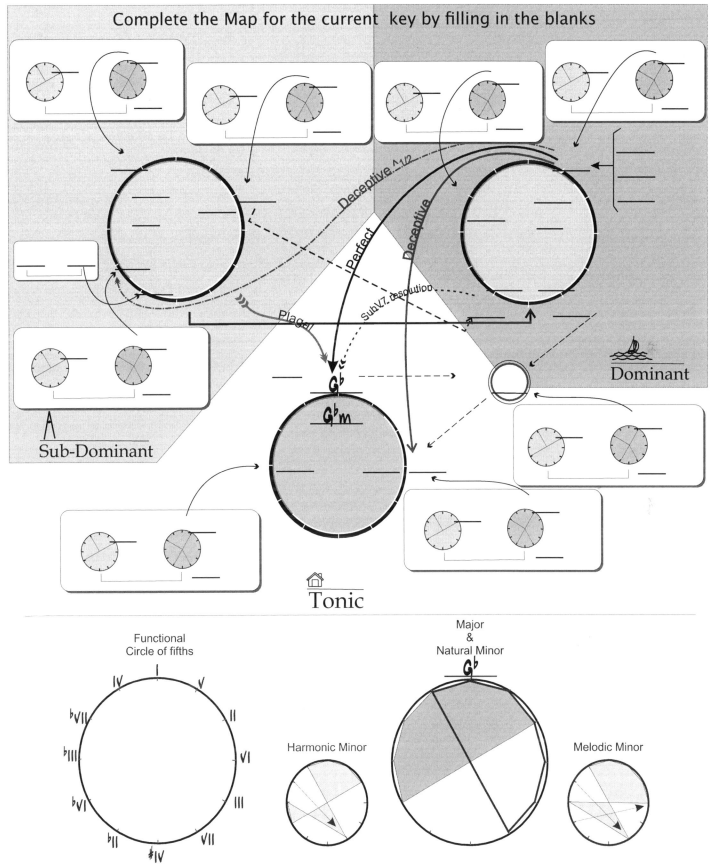

Complete the Map for the current key by filling in the blanks

Deceptive ^1/2

Deceptive

Perfect

SubbV7 resolution

Plagal

A
Sub-Dominant

Dominant

G♭
G♭m

🏠
Tonic

Functional
Circle of fifths

I
IV   V
ᵇVII   II
ᵇIII   VI
ᵇVI   III
ᵇII   VII
♯IV

Major
&
Natural Minor
G♭

Harmonic Minor

Melodic Minor

1

I^7	IV^7	I^7	I^7	IV^7	VII^{o7} OF V
$I/5$	V^7	IIm^7	V^7	I^7 V^7 OF II	V^7 OF V V^7

2

Im	IV^7	Im	IV^7	$\flat III$	IV
Im	IV^7	$\flat III$	IV	Im	Im

3

Im	$(IIm^7$ $V^7)$ OF $\flat II$	$\flat II$ MAJ^7	$IIm^{7\flat5}$	V^7	Im
Im	$(IIm^7$ $V^7)$ OF $\flat II$	$\flat II$ MAJ^7	V^7	Im $\flat II$ MAJ^7	I

4

I	Vm	I	Vm	I Vm	I
Im	Vm	Im	Vm	Im Vm	Im

5

I^7	$\flat VII$ IV	I	IV^7 $\flat VII$	I	$\flat VI$ $\flat VII$
I	IV^7	I^7	IV^7	I	I^7

Write down the same progressions in the current key and play them.

1

2

3

4

5

Key of G

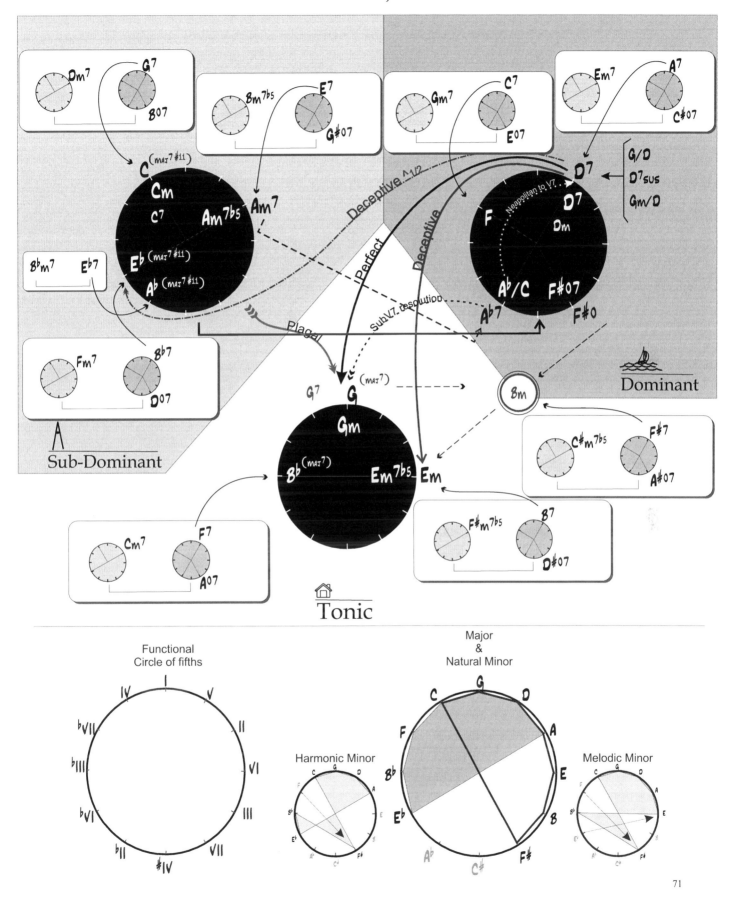

Composer's Diary
Compose your own harmonic progressions in the current key.
Include the new chords/functions introduced in this chapter.

Do not forget the clefs, key signature and meter

Key of G

Complete the Map for the current key by filling in the blanks

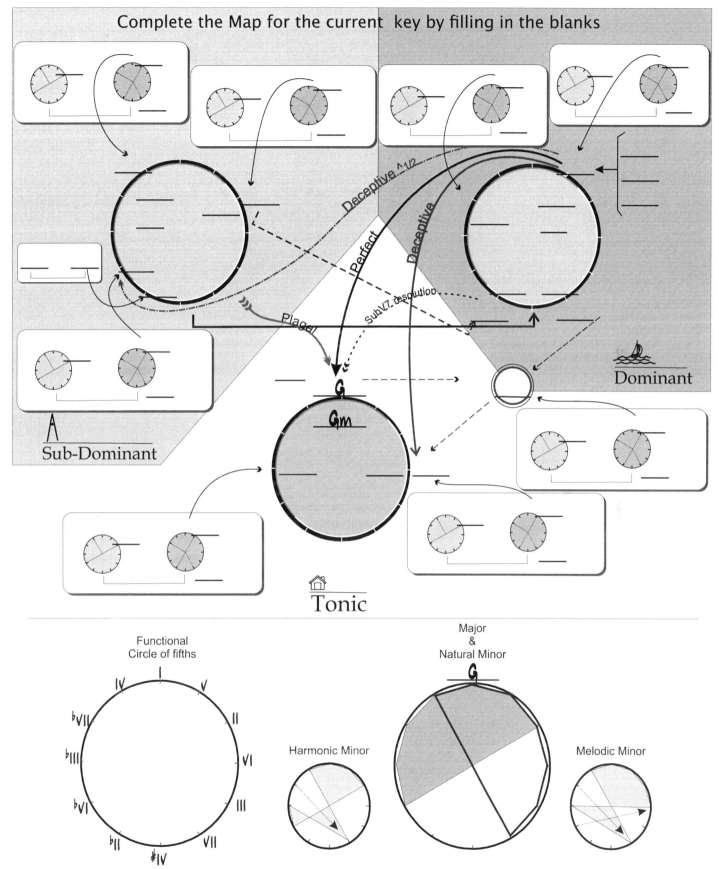

Deceptive M12

Perfect

Deceptive

Plagal

SubV7 resolution

A
Sub-Dominant

Dominant

G
Gm

Tonic

Functional
Circle of fifths

IV   I   V

♭VII   II

♭III   VI

♭VI   III

♭II   ♯IV   VII

Major
&
Natural Minor

G

Harmonic Minor

Melodic Minor

1

I^7	IV^7	I^7	I^7	IV^7	VII^{o7} of V
$I/5$	V^7	IIm^7	V^7	I^7 V^7 of II	V^7 of V V^7 ‖

2

Im	IV^7	Im	IV^7	$\flat III$	IV
Im	IV^7	$\flat III$	IV	Im	Im ‖

3

Im	$(IIm^7\ V^7)$ of $\flat II$	$\flat II\ maj^7$	$IIm^{7\flat5}$	V^7	Im
Im	$(IIm^7\ V^7)$ of $\flat II$	$\flat II\ maj^7$	V^7	$Im\ \flat II\ maj^7$	I ‖

4

I	Vm	I	Vm	$I\ Vm$	I
Im	Vm	Im	Vm	$Im\ Vm$	Im ‖

5

I^7	$\flat VII\ IV$	I	$IV^7\ \flat VII$	I	$\flat VI\ \flat VII$
I	IV^7	I^7	IV^7	I	I^7 ‖

Write down the same progressions in the current key and play them.

1

2

3

4

5

Key of G#

Mapping blues I7 IV7. Additional minor mode functions.
The bIImaj7 subdominant minor and its related IIm7-V7

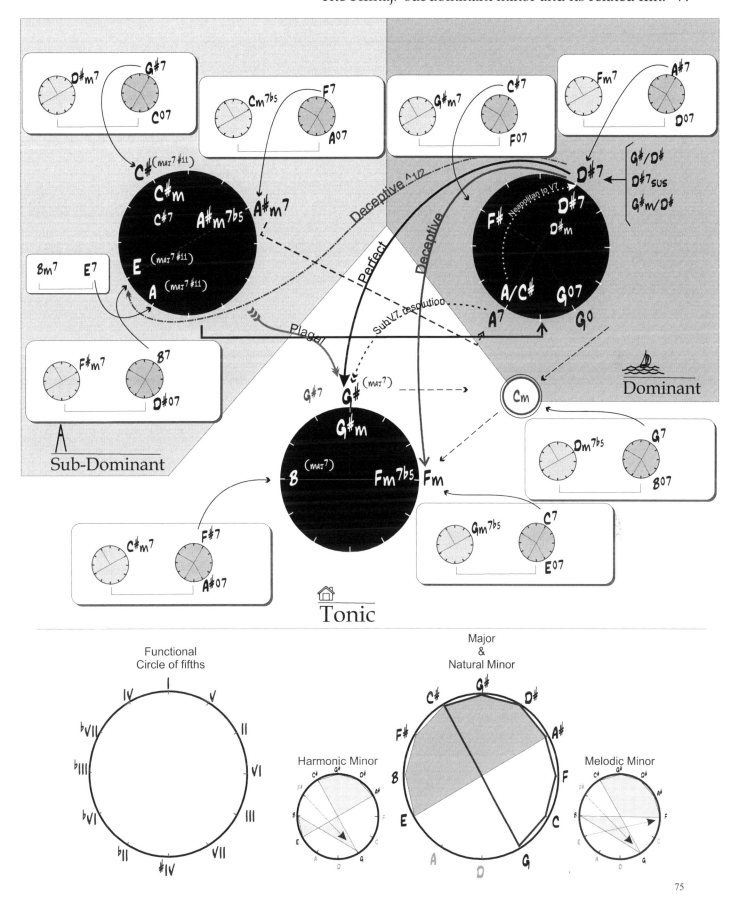

A
Sub-Dominant

Tonic

Dominant

Functional
Circle of fifths

Major
&
Natural Minor

Harmonic Minor

Melodic Minor

75

Composer's Diary

Compose your own harmonic progressions in the current key.
Include the new chords/functions introduced in this chapter.

Do not forget the clefs, key signature and meter

Mapping blues I7 IV7. Additional minor mode functions.
The bIImaj7 subdominant minor and its related IIm7-V7

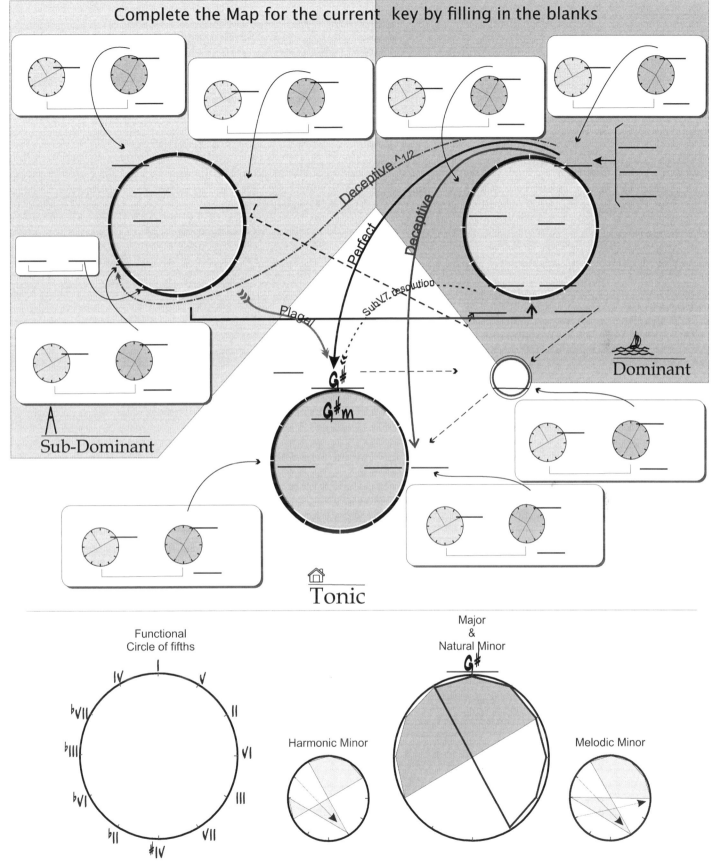

Complete the Map for the current key by filling in the blanks

Sub-Dominant

Dominant

Tonic

Functional
Circle of fifths

Major
&
Natural Minor

Harmonic Minor

Melodic Minor

1

I^7	IV^7	I^7	I^7	IV^7	VII^{o7} OF V
$I/^5$	V^7	IIm^7	V^7	I^7 V^7 OF II	V^7 OF V V^7

2

Im	IV^7	Im	IV^7	$♭III$	IV
Im	IV^7	$♭III$	IV	Im	Im

3

Im	(IIm^7 V^7) OF $♭II$	$♭II$ MAJ^7	$IIm^{7♭5}$	V^7	Im
Im	(IIm^7 V^7) OF $♭II$	$♭II$ MAJ^7	V^7	Im $♭II$ MAJ^7	I

4

I	Vm	I	Vm	I Vm	I
Im	Vm	Im	Vm	Im Vm	Im

5

I^7	$♭VII$ IV	I	IV^7 $♭VII$	I	$♭VI$ $♭VII$
I	IV^7	I^7	IV^7	I	I^7

Write down the same progressions in the current key and play them.

1

2

3

4

5

Key of A♭

Mapping blues I7 IV7. Additional minor mode functions.
The bIImaj7 subdominant minor and its related IIm7-V7

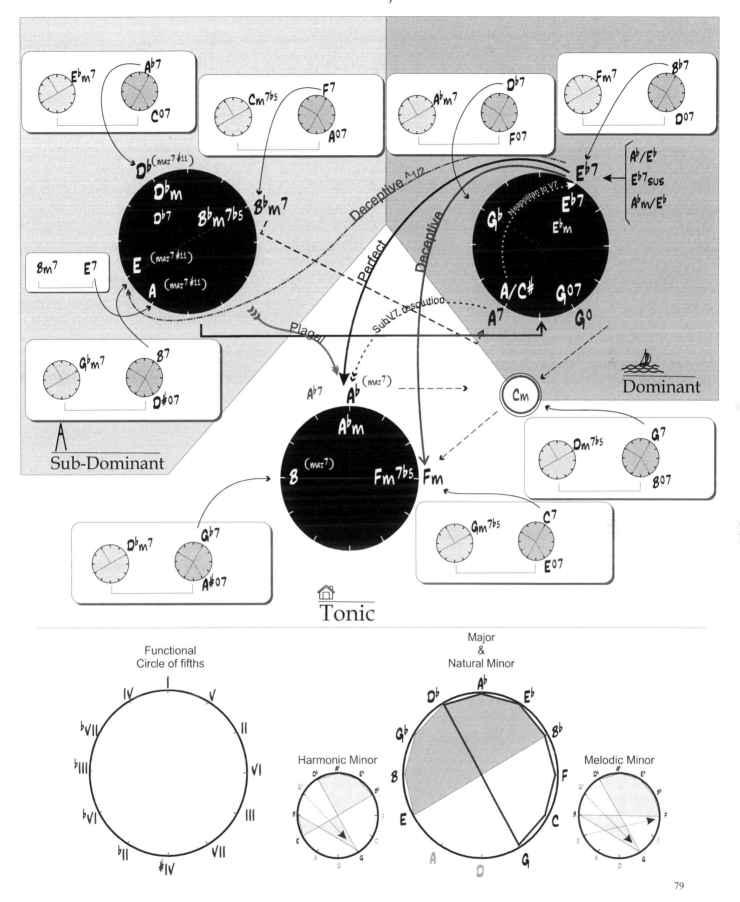

79

Composer's Diary

Compose your own harmonic progressions in the current key.
Include the new chords/functions introduced in this chapter.

Do not forget the clefs, key signature and meter

Key of A♭

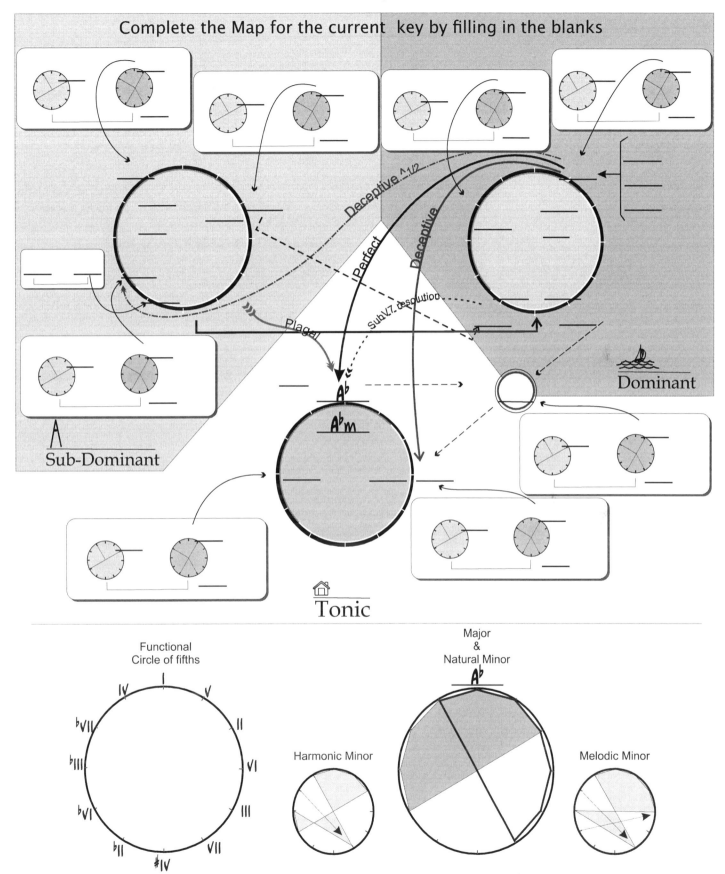

Mapping blues I7 IV7. Additional minor mode functions.
The bIImaj7 subdominant minor and its related IIm7-V7

Complete the Map for the current key by filling in the blanks

Deceptive ^1/2

Deceptive

Perfect

SubV7. resolution

Plagal

A♭

A♭m

Dominant

A
Sub-Dominant

🏠
Tonic

Functional
Circle of fifths

IV   I   V

♭VII   II

♭III   VI

♭VI   III

♭II   VII
♯IV

Harmonic Minor

Major
&
Natural Minor

A♭

Melodic Minor

81

Functional Progressions

1

I⁷	IV⁷	I⁷	I⁷	IV⁷	VII⁰⁷ ᴏꜰ V

$\text{I}^7 \mid \text{IV}^7 \mid \text{I}^7 \mid \text{I}^7 \mid \text{IV}^7 \mid \text{VII}^{07}\text{ of V}$

$\text{I}/5 \mid \text{V}^7 \mid \text{IIm}^7 \mid \text{V}^7 \mid \text{I}^7 \ \text{V}^7\text{ of II} \mid \text{V}^7\text{ of V} \ \text{V}^7 \|$

2

$\text{Im} \mid \text{IV}^7 \mid \text{Im} \mid \text{IV}^7 \mid {}^\flat\text{III} \mid \text{IV}$

$\text{Im} \mid \text{IV}^7 \mid {}^\flat\text{III} \mid \text{IV} \mid \text{Im} \mid \text{Im} \|$

3

$\text{Im} \mid (\text{IIm}^7 \ \text{V}^7)\text{ of }{}^\flat\text{II} \mid {}^\flat\text{II}\,\text{maj}^7 \mid \text{IIm}^{7\flat5} \mid \text{V}^7 \mid \text{Im}$

$\text{Im} \mid (\text{IIm}^7 \ \text{V}^7)\text{ of }{}^\flat\text{II} \mid {}^\flat\text{II}\,\text{maj}^7 \mid \text{V}^7 \mid \text{Im}\ {}^\flat\text{II}\,\text{maj}^7 \mid \text{I} \|$

4

$\text{I} \mid \text{Vm} \mid \text{I} \mid \text{Vm} \mid \text{I}\ \text{Vm} \mid \text{I}$

$\text{Im} \mid \text{Vm} \mid \text{Im} \mid \text{Vm} \mid \text{Im}\ \text{Vm} \mid \text{Im} \|$

5

$\text{I}^7 \mid {}^\flat\text{VII}\ \text{IV} \mid \text{I} \mid \text{IV}^7\ {}^\flat\text{VII} \mid \text{I} \mid {}^\flat\text{VI}\ {}^\flat\text{VII}$

$\text{I} \mid \text{IV}^7 \mid \text{I}^7 \mid \text{IV}^7 \mid \text{I} \mid \text{I}^7 \|$

Write down the same progressions in the current key and play them.

1

2

3

4

5

Key of A

Mapping blues I7 IV7. Additional minor mode functions.
The bIImaj7 subdominant minor and its related IIm7-V7

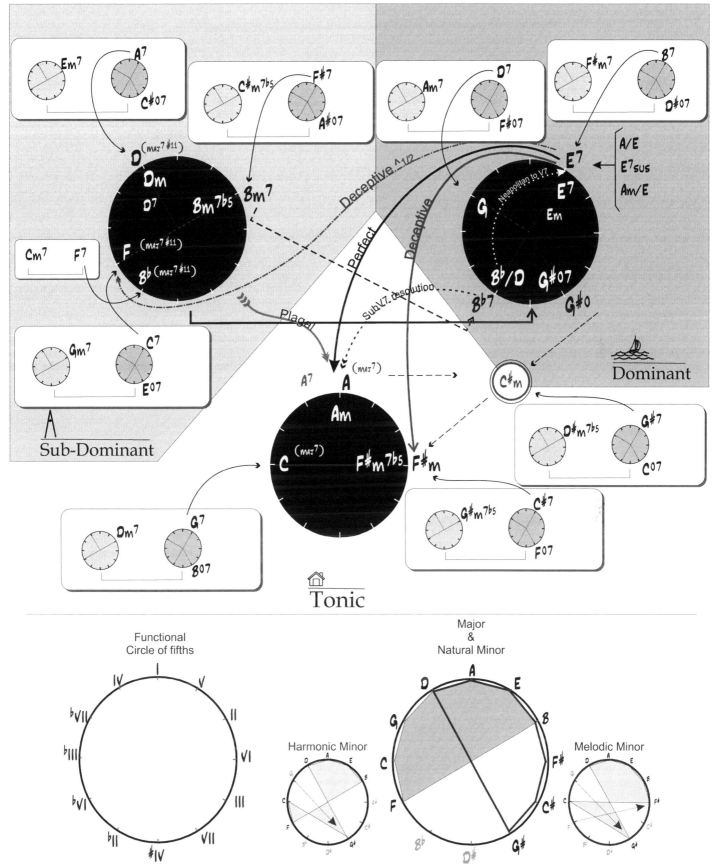

Composer's Diary

Compose your own harmonic progressions in the current key.
Include the new chords/functions introduced in this chapter.

Do not forget the clefs, key signature and meter

Key of A

Complete the Map for the current key by filling in the blanks

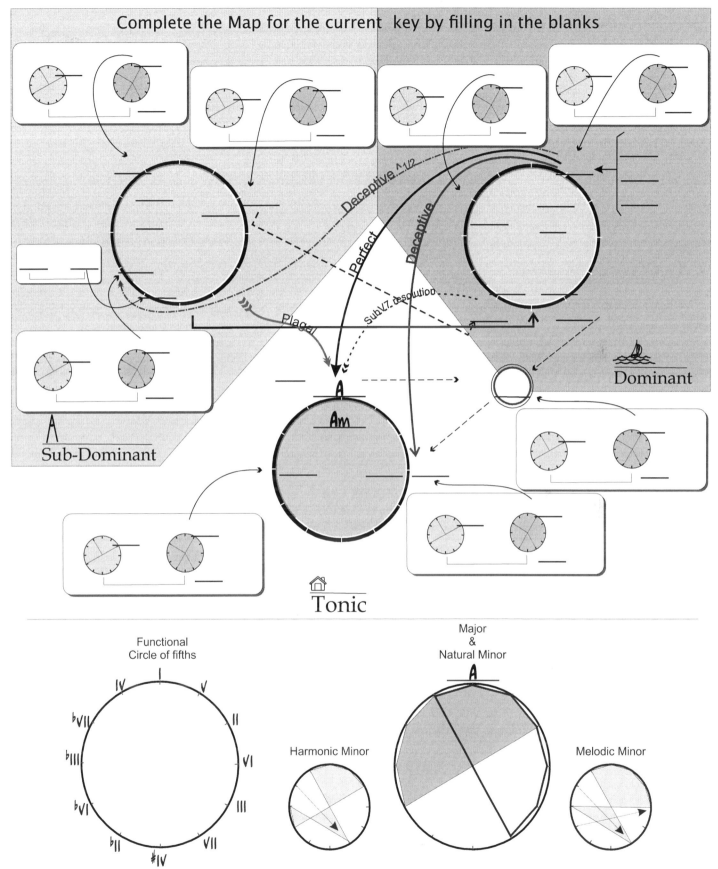

Deceptive ^1/2

Deceptive

Perfect

Plagal

SubV7. resolution

Am

Dominant

Sub-Dominant

A

Tonic

Functional
Circle of fifths

IV I V

bVII II

bIII VI

bVI III

bII VII

#IV

Major
&
Natural Minor

A

Harmonic Minor

Melodic Minor

Functional Progressions Worksheet

1

I^7	IV^7	I^7	I^7	IV^7	VII^{o7} of V
$I/5$	V^7	IIm^7	V^7	I^7 V^7 of II	V^7 of V V^7 ‖

2

Im	IV^7	Im	IV^7	^bIII	IV
Im	IV^7	^bIII	IV	Im	Im ‖

3

Im	(IIm^7 V^7) of ^bII	^bII maj^7	IIm^{7b5}	V^7	Im
Im	(IIm^7 V^7) of ^bII	^bII maj^7	V^7	Im ^bII maj^7	I ‖

4

I	Vm	I	Vm	I Vm	I
Im	Vm	Im	Vm	Im Vm	Im ‖

5

I^7	^bVII IV	I	IV^7 ^bVII	I	^bVI ^bVII
I	IV^7	I^7	IV^7	I	I^7 ‖

Write down the same progressions in the current key and play them.

1

2

3

4

5

Key of A#

Mapping blues I7 IV7. Additional minor mode functions.
The bIImaj7 subdominant minor and its related IIm7-V7

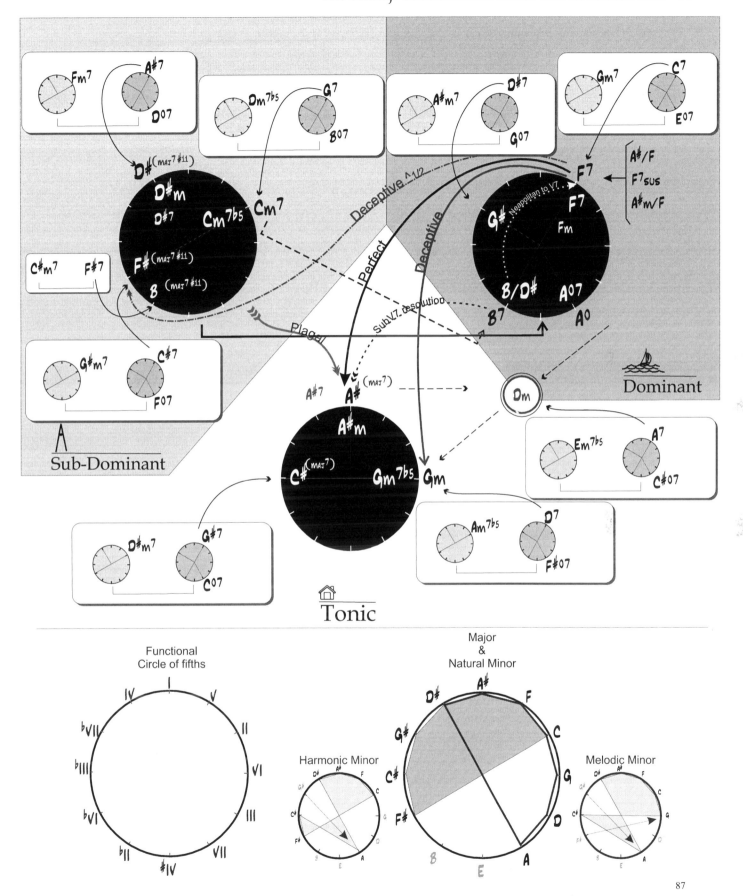

Composer's Diary

Compose your own harmonic progressions in the current key.
Include the new chords/functions introduced in this chapter.

Do not forget the clefs, key signature and meter

Key of A♯

Mapping blues I7 IV7. Additional minor mode functions.
The bIImaj7 subdominant minor and its related IIm7-V7

Complete the Map for the current key by filling in the blanks

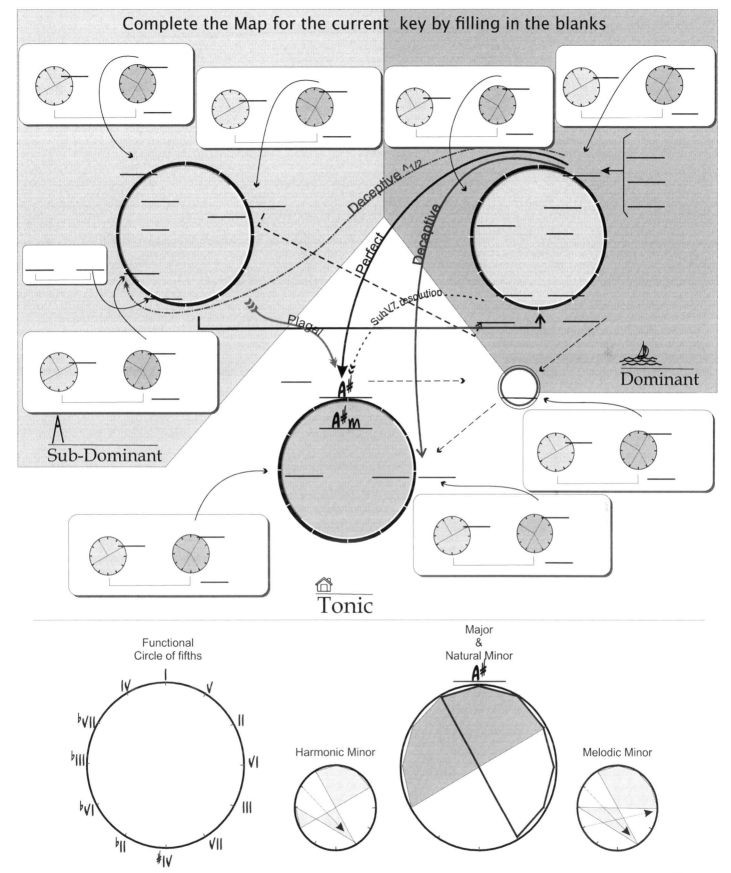

Deceptive ^1/2

Perfect

Deceptive

SubV7 resolution

Plagal

A♯

A♯m

Dominant

Sub-Dominant

Tonic

Functional
Circle of fifths

Major
&
Natural Minor

A♯

Harmonic Minor

Melodic Minor

IV   I   V

♭VII   II

♭III   VI

♭VI   III

♭II   VII

♯IV

89

Mapping blues I7 IV7. Additional minor mode functions.
The bIImaj7 subdominant minor and its related IIm7-V7

New Chords/Functions in the current level

Tonic: B♭7

Sub-Dominant: E♭7 B AND B maj7

Dominant: Fm modal Vm

Secondary: IIm7 AND V7 OF bIImaj7

Harmonic Progressions examples

B♭7	E♭7	B♭7	B♭7	E♭7	E°7
B♭/F	G7	Cm7	F7	B♭7 G7	C7 F7
B♭m	E♭7	B♭m	E♭7	D♭	E♭
B♭m	E♭7	D♭	E♭	B♭m	B♭m
B♭m	D♭m7 G♭7	B maj7	Cm7b5	F7	B♭m
B♭m	D♭m7 G♭7	B maj7	F7	B♭m B maj7	B♭
B♭	Fm	B♭	Fm	B♭ Fm	B♭
B♭m	Fm	B♭m	Fm	B♭m Fm	B♭m
B♭7	A♭ E♭	B♭	E♭7 A♭	B♭	G♭ A♭
B♭	E♭7	B♭7	E♭7	B♭	B♭7

Write down the same progressions in other keys using the map for the new key.

Concepts

More borrowed chords from other modes and paths to modulations.

The IV7 from dorian minor. The modal Vm.

The bIImaj7 subdominant minor chord (or root-altered IIm7b5) and its related

IIm7 and V7. The I7 as tonic in the Blues and Blues form.

Key of B♭

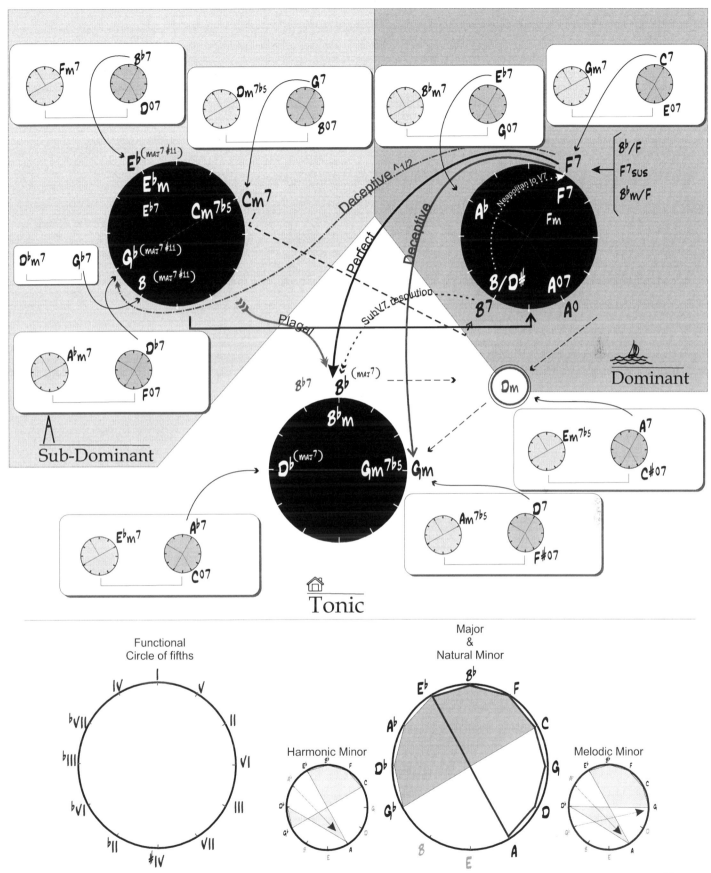

Composer's Diary

Compose your own harmonic progressions in the current key.
Include the new chords/functions introduced in this chapter.

Do not forget the clefs, key signature and meter

Key of B♭

Mapping blues I7 IV7. Additional minor mode functions.
The bIImaj7 subdominant minor and its related IIm7-V7

Complete the Map for the current key by filling in the blanks

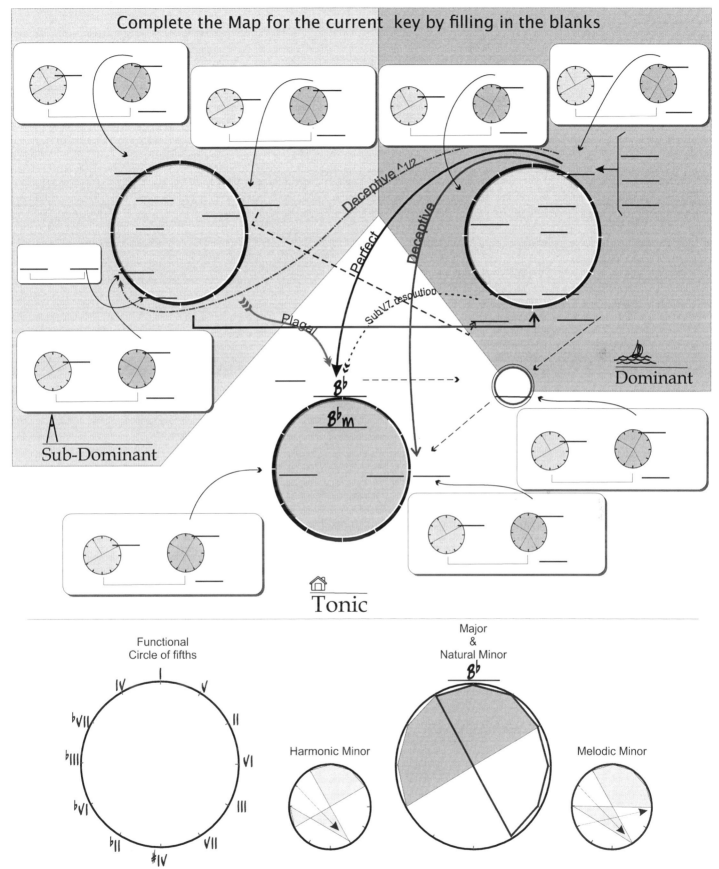

Deceptive ^1/2

Perfect

Deceptive

SubV7. resolution

Plagal

B♭

B♭m

Dominant

Sub-Dominant

Tonic

Functional
Circle of fifths

IV · I · V · II · VI · III · VII · #IV · bII · bVI · bIII · bVII

Major
&
Natural Minor
B♭

Harmonic Minor

Melodic Minor

93

Functional Progressions

1

I^7	IV^7	I^7	I^7	IV^7	VII^{o7} OF V
$I/5$	V^7	IIm^7	V^7	I^7 V^7 OF II	V^7 OF V V^7

2

Im	IV^7	Im	IV^7	$\flat III$	IV
Im	IV^7	$\flat III$	IV	Im	Im

3

Im	(IIm^7 V^7) OF $\flat II$	$\flat II$ MAJ^7	$IIm^{7\flat5}$	V^7	Im
Im	(IIm^7 V^7) OF $\flat II$	$\flat II$ MAJ^7	V^7	Im $\flat II$ MAJ^7	I

4

I	Vm	I	Vm	I Vm	I
Im	Vm	Im	Vm	Im Vm	Im

5

I^7	$\flat VII$ IV	I	IV^7 $\flat VII$	I	$\flat VI$ $\flat VII$
I	IV^7	I^7	IV^7	I	I^7

Write down the same progressions in the current key and play them.

1

2

3

| | | | | | |

4

5

Key of B

Mapping blues I7 IV7. Additional minor mode functions.
The bIImaj7 subdominant minor and its related IIm7-V7

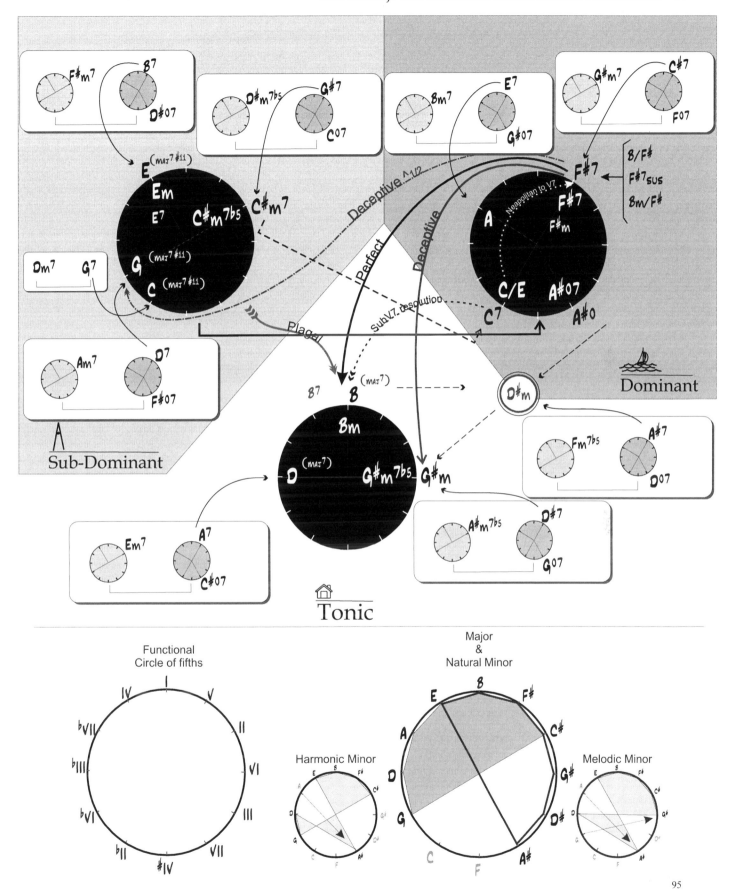

Composer's Diary

Compose your own harmonic progressions in the current key.
Include the new chords/functions introduced in this chapter.

Do not forget the clefs, key signature and meter

Key of B

Complete the Map for the current key by filling in the blanks

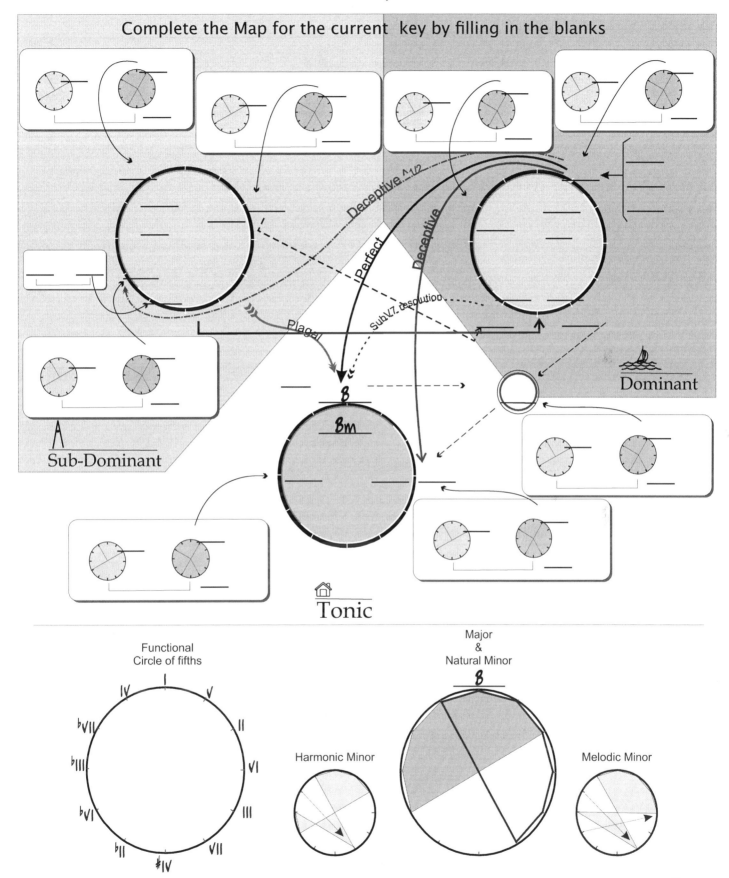

Deceptive ^1/2

Deceptive

Perfect

Plagal

SubV7 resolution

Dominant

B

Bm

A
Sub-Dominant

🏠
Tonic

Functional
Circle of fifths

IV — I — V
bVII — II
bIII — VI
bVI — III
bII — VII
#IV

Major
&
Natural Minor

B

Harmonic Minor

Melodic Minor

Other Books in the mDecks Series

146629101
UST Jazz Piano Chord Voicings Vol. 1
Individual Upper Structure Triads over IIm7 and V7

UST Jazz Piano Chord Voicings Vol. 1 is part of the complete method to study and learn all possible Upper Structure Triad Voicings over the IIm7 and V7.

1441412166
Piano Technique Vol. 1
Finger Control
Independence, balance and strength
Rhythmic subivisions and essential Polyrhythms

Piano Technique Vol.1 consists of 46 exercises, covering two main technical challenges for the piano player. Playing the piano requires the use of very fine dexterity. To acquire such skill, the brain must be challenged consistently and repeatedly by the same proposals, causing a self-induced restructuring. This transformation is not a trivial one, and it only comes to be after all the necessary work has been done and sufficient amount of time is invested.

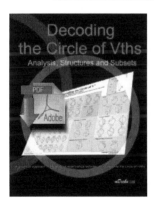

Decoding the Circle of V^{ths}
Analysis, Structures and Subsets

A graphical approach in the study of relationships between structures over the circle of fifths.

From jazz improvisation and voicings to tonal and atonal music composition and theory, many exercises and studies can be designed using this graphical approach to musical structures over the circle of fifths.

Check for these and more at **www.mDecks.com**

Made in the USA
San Bernardino, CA
26 November 2014